Charles John Vaughan

Lessons of the Cross and Passion

Six lectures delivered in Hereford cathedral during the week before

Easter, 1869

Charles John Vaughan

Lessons of the Cross and Passion
Six lectures delivered in Hereford cathedral during the week before Easter, 1869

ISBN/EAN: 9783337253868

Printed in Europe, USA, Canada, Australia, Japan

Cover: Foto ©Lupo / pixelio.de

More available books at **www.hansebooks.com**

LESSONS OF THE CROSS AND PASSION:

SIX LECTURES

DELIVERED IN HEREFORD CATHEDRAL DURING THE
WEEK BEFORE EASTER, 1869.

BY

C. J. VAUGHAN, D.D.

VICAR OF DONCASTER.

PUBLISHED BY REQUEST.

London and Cambridge:
MACMILLAN AND CO.
1869.

TO THE

HONOURABLE AND VERY REVEREND

GEORGE HERBERT, M.A.

DEAN OF HEREFORD,

THESE LECTURES

DELIVERED BY HIS APPOINTMENT

AND NOW PUBLISHED AT HIS DESIRE

ARE DEDICATED

WITH GRATEFUL AND RESPECTFUL REMEMBRANCE.

CONTENTS.

I.

TOO LATE.

St MATTHEW XXVI. 45.

Sleep on now, and take your rest . . . PAGE 1

II.

THE DIVINE SACRIFICE AND THE HUMAN PRIESTHOOD.

HEBREWS X. 19—22.

Having therefore, brethren, boldness to enter into the holiest by the blood of Jesus, by a new and living way, which He hath consecrated for us, through the veil, that is to say, His flesh; and having an High Priest over the house of God; let us draw near with a true heart in full assurance of faith, having our hearts sprinkled from an evil conscience, and our bodies washed with pure water . 15

III.

LOVE NOT THE WORLD.

1 JOHN ii. 15.

Love not the world . . . 29

IV.

THE MORAL GLORY OF CHRIST.

JOHN i. 14.

And we beheld His glory . 46

V.

CHRIST MADE PERFECT THROUGH SUFFERING.

HEBREWS II. 10.

It became Him, for whom are all things, and by whom are all things, in bringing many sons unto glory, to make the Captain of their salvation perfect through sufferings . 62

VI.

DEATH THE REMEDY OF CHRIST'S LONELINESS.

ST JOHN XII. 24.

Verily, verily, I say unto you, Except a corn of wheat fall into the ground and die, it abideth alone: but if it die, it bringeth forth much fruit 77

I.

TOO LATE.

ST MATTHEW XXVI. 45.

Sleep on now, and take your rest.

THE first sound of the words is reposeful and comforting. *I will lay me down in peace, and take my rest—so He giveth His beloved sleep—yea, thou shalt lie down, and thy sleep shall be sweet—Lord, if he sleep, he shall do well*—these are the ideas connected, even in the Bible, with that natural repose, that *taking of rest in sleep,* which almost divides with work itself this lifetime of responsible being.

But when we look below the surface, when we remember the time and the place and the circumstances, when we think of the Speaker of the words and of the persons spoken to, we shall perceive that the command —for such it seems to be—*Sleep on and take your rest,* had a widely different meaning from that which its sound would convey.

This was the very night on which Christ was betrayed. Already He has taken His last earthly meal, and refused to drink, even that night, of the fruit of the vine. He has done with earth, except as a suffering-place. He has gone forth with His Disciples to that sequestered garden whither the traitor disciple is about to track Him. *Exceeding sorrowful, even unto death*[1], He has thrown Himself, as it were, upon the sympathy, almost upon the compassion, of His three chief Friends, to keep awake with Him through His agony. *Tarry ye here*, He said, *and watch with me.* In vain. Grief itself has made them drowsy. *Sleeping for sorrow*[2] is the description of them as He comes back from His solitary wrestling to seek that fellowship which was His only earthly solace. Again and again He has reproved this sleep, even while in His tenderness He made excuse for it. *What, could ye not watch with me one hour? Watch and pray, that ye enter not into temptation: the spirit indeed is willing, but the flesh is weak.* Therefore, when He comes at last to them and says, *Sleep on now, and take your rest;* and when, almost in the same breath with this permission, with this command, to sleep, He adds, as though in direct contradiction to it, *Rise, let us be going*—and explains the summons by saying, *He is at hand that doth betray me;* we are obliged to look for something more and other in the saying than its literal sense. If we had been reading of a merely human actor, we should have called it irony: we should have thought it almost the language of banter or mockery, to bid persons in the same breath to *sleep on* and to *rise*

---

[1] Matt. xxvi. 38.   [2] Luke xxii. 45.

and be going: as we are reading the words of One who never speaks in sarcasm, we must conclude that here, as everywhere, He is teaching something by this seeming discrepancy between the two parts of the sentence— something which it becomes us reverently to study and humbly to learn.

And we shall find the lesson a very sad one. God grant that we may not have to receive it, now or at any time, as applicable, in its deepest sadness, to ourselves!

The Disciples were about to enter into temptation. Satan, as they had been warned at the Table, had *desired* them, had *demanded* or *begged*[1] them—even as of old he asked of God the holy Patriarch[2]—that he might sift them as wheat. For the enemy too, like Christ[3], has his winnowing-fan: and that which in God's hand is trial, is in the devil's hand temptation. Who has not known it? that searching, piercing, exploring process, by which sin finds us out, and compels us to show, in shame perhaps and ignominy, the inherent weakness of the creature, the absolute nothingness of the fallen? It was so with the Disciples that night. They were to be explored, put under the devil's winnowing-fan, that he might separate chaff from wheat, and show them what they were.

Christ had warned them. Again and again He had told them what that night was to be to them. And now, withdrawn with them, in that night scene, in that lonely garden, He had impressed upon them again and again

---
[1] Luke xxii. 31. [2] Job i. 11, 12. ii. 5, 6.
[3] Matt. iii. 12.

the necessity of wakeful prayer. There is a watching, there is a praying, always seasonable: there is also a special watching, in the prospect of special trial: and here Christ Himself bids them practise it. They fail. They suffer the weakness of the flesh to prevail over the willingness of the spirit. They sleep while Christ watches. They suffer Him to come to them in vain, twice over, to summon them to duty. The first time, and again the second time, *He finds them sleeping.* When He comes the third time, He says not, *Watch and pray*— He says,
>*Sleep on now, and take your rest.*

We see what He means. He means, *It is too late now. The opportunity is lost and gone. The time for watching and praying is over: you have let it escape you. You may as well sleep now: alas! there is now nothing to be done: you must now enter, as you may, into temptation: it must wrap you all round, you must breathe it, you must have it as near you as the light and air: all unarmed, all naked and defenceless, because you would not watch and pray, you must now resign yourself to the unequal encounter, and take what comes. Sleep on now, if you can, and take your rest: the soul at least can sleep— that is always possible: with sleeping souls then, if in waking bodies, rise, and meet the foe!*

If this be the true account of the words as first spoken, we shall readily think of ways in which they come home to us.

1. They have a direct bearing upon the whole subject of *Temptation.* Is there one here present who scoffs

at the word temptation? Has the infidelity of the day infected you with doubts as to the existence of an evil spirit? Have any of us asked the caviller's question, How can the devil tempt? how can one spirit have access to another spirit, so as to breathe a thought or arouse a purpose of evil?

Even you will scarcely doubt the existence of human tempters. What foul sin done upon this earth has not been suggested, has not certainly been prepared for, by what we call, speaking very generally, *influence*—the flowing in, that is, of something which was once without the man—not his own originally, but another's? Of all ruined lives, of all corrupted destroyed souls—alas! you know that they are many—which has been ruined, spoilt, destroyed, quite alone, quite of itself? Which is not at least as much a victim as an agent in the ruin? Mind has acted upon mind, spirit upon spirit: in some mysterious manner, soul does touch soul, for good or for evil: there is some attraction, some magnetism, some spell and fascination, between being and being, quite apart— in many cases, quite apart—from the body: in ten thousand instances this out-flowing and in-flowing, this effluence and this influence, is altogether mental: it helps me to realize what Scripture says of our *wrestling not against flesh and blood*, but against evil spirits: tenants of the air St Paul calls them[1], as though to guard us against a fatal security—as though to warn us that they are as near to us as the air we breathe—as near and as impalpable too!

[1] Compare Eph. ii. 2. vi. 12.

But for the present purpose it is enough if we draw even upon the experience of human temptations. Even those trials which the disciples were to undergo that night of the Passion—those which Christ spoke of as coming upon them from the devil—even these came through human agencies: *the maid who kept the door* was a human tempter when she said to Peter, *Thou also art one of them:* it was under that temptation that Peter fell, and the influence which made it a temptation was subtler and more spiritual than the form. So it is with our temptations. They too come to us, in large part, through human beings. Let us think of these.

We are warned to expect them. No man passes through life—no man passes into life—without encountering temptation. If not of this kind, then (for that very reason) of another kind; just because the disposition makes that a temptation, when this would not be. To all therefore, Christ says—to all, young and old—to all, rich and poor, one with another—*Watch and pray, lest ye enter into temptation.* Temptation is a peril. It must either be great suffering—it is so to those who overcome —it was so even to Christ—He, it is written, *suffered being tempted*[1]—or worse. Temptation yielded to, temptation victorious, is sin: *and sin, when it is finished, brings forth death*[2]. Therefore Christ, who loves us, and who came to save, bids us to watch and pray lest we enter into temptation.

This, beforehand. The traitor was not yet in sight with his band and his weapons. The High Priest's

[1] Heb. ii. 18.   [2] James i. 15.

servants, who were to be the human tempters, were themselves sleeping unconscious. This is the time for watching and praying. Before the temptation comes. Mark that well. It is the moral of the whole. Some will pray, or think that they pray, as they enter into temptation. And Prayer is good at all times. But, remember, there is a prayer which comes too late: there is a prayer which even contradicts itself in the asking: there is a prayer which asks to be kept safe under a temptation which we are going in quest of. That is not the watching and praying of which Christ speaks. To be of use, prayer must precede temptation; must arm and fence the man who is to be tempted, with that *whole armour of God*, one part of which is *Praying always*[1]. The man who earnestly puts himself into the hands of God *betimes in the morning;* the man who strives to maintain throughout the day the spirit of wakefulness and upward-looking; he is the man who will be kept in that *hour of temptation which shall come on all the world*[2]: he is the man who, whether his Lord come late or come early, shall be found, when He cometh, watching, and therefore blessed.

But if we will not pray before temptation; if we will rely upon good intentions, which are unstable as water; or upon a probable freedom from temptation, which may or may not be to-day, and which cannot be always; then there comes a moment, at which Christ Himself must look upon us and say, *Too late. Sleep on now, and take*

[1] Eph. vi. 18. [2] Rev. iii. 10.

your rest: the enemy is upon you now, and only they shall stand who were armed in the armour of God beforehand.

There is a prayer, there is a watching, which comes too late in reference to temptation. He who would not obey Christ's call, when He came, twice over, to bid him watch unto prayer, must expect to have the words spoken to him, when temptation itself is upon him, *You may as well sleep on now and take your rest. Now you have entered into temptation.* The very atmosphere is charged with it. It enters at eye and ear, it enters at nostril and mouth. You are an infected man. The prayer which would rise from you now, like Peter's prayer in the High Priest's kitchen, is foul with the poison which you deprecate. Too late —too late. The only chance for you now is through repentance, through bitter tears and agonized recollections. *When thou art converted—then, not before—when thou art converted, strengthen thy brethren.*

2. *Sleep on now, and take your rest.* The words have a meaning also, as respects *Opportunity*. The opportunities of life are many. Life itself is a wonderful thing: not least in this—in its opportunities. O how much may we do, the least of us, in this our day! Show me the man, the woman, the child, who has no influence! I shall ask many questions before I believe that there is one such! There are parents, perhaps, here to-night who would not have been here but for their children! Christ says to each of us, in reference to opportunity, *Watch and pray*. Are we willing? Who has not slept, in this matter, when he ought to have been waking? Who has not suffered minds, characters, lives, souls, to

escape from that influence for good which he himself, small as he is, might have exercised? Who has not cause to reproach himself, when he compares that which he has done with that which he might have done, in this one matter—of opportunity?

God gives us all a multitude of opportunities, and with respect to all He says to us, *Watch and pray. Occupy till I come.* We will not. We never see, never feel, the sacred aspect of these things. Each opportunity as it is towards God, is also, as towards man, a possibility of selfishness. There is not a relation in which we stand one to another, which may not be taken as a selfishness and refused as an opportunity. One by one, these are withdrawn. He who once said, *Watch and pray*, says at last, *Sleep on now, and take your rest.*

It is so with us, when we stand by the open grave, and lay in it, to be no more seen, the body of father or mother, of wife or child or friend. Ill used or well, the opportunity is gone by. We can do no more now, for ever, in reference to that relationship. I find it hard to conceive of that loss, of that severance, of that bereavement, of which this is not the chief ingredient of the bitterness. *Sleep on now*, sleep for ever, so far as regards that friend, that living soul, which was once so much to thee. No more can be done now, nothing ever again, to soothe one aching of that heart, or to slake one thirsting of that soul. That parent who was so often vexed and grieved by thy coldness, by thy unkindness, by thy disobedience, can never henceforth know thee as a strength or a consolation. That companion, dear to thee as thy soul, and, alas! not more regarded; neglected, like that, as to all interests which can survive death; cheated, like that, of all influence which God claimed from thee towards him, and now finally buried out of thy sight—concerning him too the words are sadly, frightfully true for thee, *Sleep on now,* sleep for ever, *and take thy rest.* Too late, too late—alike the warning which might once have repelled from evil, and the persuasion which might have attracted towards the thing that is good.

So is it with regard to all the several opportunities of which life is made up. There is a time during which to watch and pray is to be safe, to be useful, to be happy: there is a time also, in each instance, when we might as well sleep on and take our rest. Such an opportunity is Education; in the more limited sense, in which it means the training of the youth; and in the larger and more extended sense, in which it includes the whole discipline of a lifetime. Such an opportunity is the possession of a Ministry, of a Church, of a Bible, of a Gospel. God gives us each for use: Christ says to us concerning each one, *Watch and pray.* No one of all these can last for ever. A pure and vigorous Ministry seldom lasts in one Parish beyond a generation: the Bible lasts, the Gospel lasts, but not the possessor, not the user: upon him lies the responsibility of wakeful listening, of deep pondering, of anxious profiting; for soon must the one charge be exchanged for the other—*Watch and pray* for *Sleep on now and take thy rest.*

How will the recollection of each day's neglect, of

Bibles unread and Sacraments despised, of every Sermon heard idly, heard contemptuously, heard in vain, arise as if from the dust to reproach and trouble us! How shall we wish, vainly wish, that again we might hear, if so be we might yet awaken, ere it be too late, from the death of sin to that life of righteousness which is the life of God!

3. *Sleep on now, and take your rest.* The saying which is so true and so solemn as to the several opportunities which God here gives us, is not less so in its bearing upon that total sum of all opportunities, which is the *Life*.

Suppose the day at last come, which is to take us from among the living.

How often has Christ said to us, while we were still in the body, *Watch and pray!* How often has Christ come back to us, as it were, from His mediatorial work—from that *business of His Father*, that office of Redemption and Mediation, of which He spoke, in early Boyhood, as (in one part or another) His natural, His necessary occupation[1]—to arouse us from our sloth and lethargy and earthly-mindedness by the question, *Could ye not watch with me one hour*—not even that one brief hour, as it will hereafter seem to us, during which we were bidden by Him to tarry here below and share His sorrow? Often has He come and asked us this question. He has come in blessing, in the hour of joy and gladness, bidding us not to forget the Benefactor in the gift. He has come in sorrow, He has come in distress,

[1] Luke ii. 49.

He has come to us in bereavement—if by any means He might lighten our eyes that we sleep not the sleep of death[1]. He has come, and He has questioned us, in the still small voice of conscience and of the Spirit: He has come in the chastening of night, and in the solemn grandeur of the mid-day—He has come in this form and in that, He has come as the Crucified One, He has come as the Risen, He has come as the Refiner and the Purifier[2], He has come as the Rebuker and as the Judge: always with this intent, that He might impress upon us the duty of watching and the blessedness of prayer— that He might make us willing to take upon us His easy yoke, and to learn of Him the blessedness of His own Spirit. He has come, and we could not always be unconscious that He was near and that He was speaking. We might have seen, had we looked, that His countenance was sad for us and His soul sorrowful: He came to us from an intercession which cannot be joyful, while it is offered for souls still sorely jeopardized and (worse yet) unconscious still or still reluctant. He stood, and He pleaded with us concerning His sufferings; reminded us of His Agony, His Cross, His Passion, His Grave; pleaded with us, by the argument of these things, that sin must be ruin, that its wages must be death. And we would not hear. We thought that an hour or two could not matter; that life was long before us, and that either God would not be extreme to mark misdoing, or else (more wicked thought still) that that blood of which Christ spoke to us could easily wash it out. And thus

---

[1] Psalm xiii. 3.   [2] Mal. iii. 3.

we procrastinated: we dallied with Christ: we parleyed with the tempter: and though Christ came back once and again to us, He still, still, found us sleeping.

We were sorry to sleep—we thought so. And He seemed half to understand it. He was willing to believe that, though the flesh was weak, yet the spirit, surely, was ready: for *He knows our frame, and He remembers that we are but dust*[1]. We turned His gentleness, His long-suffering, His great patience, into an excuse for further trifling, for *continuing in sin* (though we called it not by that name)—we slept on, still slept, with Christ in sight, Christ in His agony, Christ on His cross, Christ in His glory.

There is an end to these things—or Christ would not be true. There is an end. We know one part of it —the outward part: the fact of death, and its nearness, and its universality: we see one another die, we expect to die—we say so, we know it—yet we sleep on.

When Christ at last comes—the third time, the Gospel story, which is also a Gospel parable, calls it, but, as concerning the thing signified, rather for the thousandth, the ten thousandth time—and finds us still sleeping; then He is compelled to say—else He could be trifled with, else He were not God, He were not the Judge, He were not the Faithful One and the True—He is compelled to say, *Sleep on now, and take your rest.* The time is gone by. *The harvest is past, the summer is ended, and we are not saved*[2]. Sleep indeed, rest, is not the word for that which comes after death to the impenitent and the unsaved—any more

---

[1] Psalm ciii. 14.   [2] Jer. viii. 20.

than it was the real thing to which the disciples were called, when it was said to them in the same breath, *Rise and be going—the traitor is here!* It is the language of sadness, of hopelessness, of despair: it is the *Too late* of a lost life—the *Too late, too late,* of a boundless eternity.

God grant us all grace to awaken this night to reflection, to penitence, to newness of life! *By Thy Cross and Passion—by Thy precious Death, by Thy glorious Resurrection—in all time of our tribulation, in all time of our wealth, in the hour of our death, in the day of our judgment—*

Good Lord,
Good Lord,
deliver us!

Sunday next before Easter,
March 21, 1869.

II.

THE DIVINE SACRIFICE AND THE HUMAN PRIESTHOOD.

Hebrews x. 19—22.

Having therefore, brethren, boldness to enter into the holiest by the blood of Jesus, by a new and living way, which He hath consecrated for us, through the veil, that is to say, His flesh; and having an High Priest over the house of God; let us draw near with a true heart in full assurance of faith, having our hearts sprinkled from an evil conscience, and our bodies washed with pure water.

Surely this passage is the very key-note of the thought, and feeling, and worship too, of Passion Week. We cannot wait for it till Good Friday, when we shall read it in the Epistle: we must go for it now. For what is our one risk, our one fear and peril, in the celebrations, at once mournful and consolatory, which have gathered or are to gather us from so many homes and occupations at this holy season? Is it not this? lest we should look upon the Agony, and the Passion, and the Cross, and the Grave, with sadness indeed, with grief, almost with horror, for the suffering endured, for the wrong done, for the holy soul wrung, and the Divine Man outraged—but without taking it home to ourselves either in its cause or in its consequence? lest we should gaze upon the spectacle and shut our eyes to its deep mystery, to its solemn admonition, to its healing comfort; saying indeed, *Was there ever sorrow like unto this sorrow?* but failing to ponder the accompanying question, *Is it nothing to you, all ye that pass by*[1]?

Now the text tells us that that sight of anguish and shame was something, is something, to each one of us; more than any other event that ever took place upon the earth; more real, more concerning, more vital, to each one here present, than any most bitter, most joyous experience, that ever changed a life or reversed the destiny of a soul. If we can only enter into this one exhortation, we shall find Passion Week not a form but a substance, and we shall go forth from it servants and soldiers of the Crucified One, no longer in name only, but in deed and in truth.

The Epistle to the Hebrews may be described as the Gospel of the Old Testament. It teaches us how every act of God from the beginning of time had a direct view to Christ; how the Law itself, in its most obscure, least spiritual, most ceremonial parts, was a very Gospel written beforehand in type and shadow, quickening a hope afterwards to be fulfilled, and bearing witness to the profound maxim of St James the Lord's Brother, *Known unto God are all His works from the beginning of the world*[2].

---

[1] Lam. i. 12. [2] Acts xv. 18.

The Epistle had, like every Book of Scripture, a direct practical object for those to whom it was sent. A tremendous crisis was at hand for its first readers. The stroke of Divine Providence, acting (as usual) through human agency, was about to fell to the ground the sturdy oak of Judaism, to level the altar of its sacrifices, and to render the Levitical worship henceforth an impossibility for the Israelite. When that time came, would the Hebrew Christian—this was the question—accept the Divine omen? Would he see God's hand in this demolition of what was once God's handywork? Would he be willing to give up his country for his faith, and the strong tie of Patriotism for the one stronger obligation of fidelity to his Spiritual King?

This Epistle came to him, on the very eve of this terrible choice and crisis, to echo in his ears the momentous word—

CHRIST IS ALL!

He is more than created Angel, He is more than human Lawgiver or Mediator, He is more than mortal Priest or Intercessor—He is more than Tabernacle or Temple, He is more than Altar or Mercy-seat, He is more than Offering or Sacrifice: having Him, you are rich in destitution; losing Him, you may get all and have nothing: follow Him, He is your Saviour; cleave to Him, He is your Life.

With the first words of the text, the Apostle, leaving doctrine, enters upon its application. He has dwelt upon the everlasting tenure of Christ's Priesthood, and contrasted it with the transferable, everchanging priesthoods of dying men. He has dwelt upon the place of Christ's ministration, not an earthly tabernacle, but the very Presence of God in Heaven. He has dwelt upon the intrinsic value of Christ's Sacrifice, as needing, as capable of, neither repetition, nor addition, nor fulfilment, inasmuch as by it, once offered, *He has perfected for ever them that are sanctified*[1].

And now, by a striking and even startling adaptation of his argument, he proceeds to say this—

In virtue of the one Divine Sacrifice, you too are Priests. You also, the whole body of common Christians, are *an holy priesthood*, ordained *to offer up spiritual sacrifices*[2]. More still than this. Each one of you is not only a subordinate Priest, like those of the Levitical order, occupied in certain ministrations about the Tabernacle and the Altar, yet excluded from its highest office of all, and from its innermost and most sacred shrine: each one of you is, in his own person, a High Priest; each one of you is called to do in his own person a thing which, under the Law, only the one High Priest was permitted to do—to take with him, not in his hand but in his heart, the blood of the one all-availing Sacrifice, and, in virtue of this passport, to penetrate through the veil, into the immediate Presence of God Himself, *with a true heart, and in full assurance of faith*.

To understand this precept thoroughly, we must go back to the Book of Leviticus, and to the ceremonies of the great Day of Expiation on the 10th day of the 7th month[3].

[1] Heb. x. 14. [2] 1 Pet. ii. 5. [3] Lev. xvi. 1, &c.

That was the one only day of the whole year, on which any human eye or foot was suffered to pass within the mysterious veil which hung between the two chambers of the Tabernacle.

On that day the High Priest alone, in garments of solemn humiliation, was directed to enter twice within the dividing curtain, first with the blood of a sin-offering for himself, and then secondly with the blood of a sin-offering for the people. On that one only day of all the year, he, alone of his generation, saw the Holiest Place of all, in which stood the Ark with its contents—the actual Decalogue, the Ten Words of God's commandment, graven on tablets of stone—and a few other wonderful records of the sojourn of Israel in the wilderness[1]; records of unbelief and murmuring, changed by God's power into memorials of His Omnipotent grace and presence.

The Apostle tells us that all this minuteness of ordinance had a meaning. I myself find it easier to believe that it had a meaning than that it had none. If God had anything at all to do with that first Dispensation, I can more readily suppose that He arranged it with a view to something than with a view to nothing. If the blood spoken of was a type of Christ's Blood, and if the Holy of Holies was a type of God's Presence in Heaven, there is a warrant, at once, for many things which otherwise I might have thought trivial or arbitrary.

The Apostle says that it was so. *The Holy Ghost,* he says, *this signifying*[2]—the Holy Ghost, with whom it is equally easy to teach by word or by sign, designing to ex-

---

[1] Heb. ix. 4.   [2] Heb. ix. 8.

press this, by a visible token, to a carnal and unspiritual age—that there was a difficulty, an obstacle somewhere to the free access of the sinful to the Holy One; a difficulty and an obstacle which must be allowed to press heavily for a time upon the conscience and heart of mankind, until in due course God should explain Himself, and teach a desiring but excluded soul how to seek Him acceptably—how to find access, and how to maintain the access once found, to the Presence and Mercy-seat of its God.

And now God has explained Himself.

Is it possible that there is any one person here present who does not care to be told how he can draw nigh to God? I trust not! Is not this the thing which presses upon the soul of a sinner—and *there is no man who sinneth not*[1]—how he can get through that Veil, that heavy massive curtain, which hangs between him and the pure Heaven where God is?

You have heard and read, again and again, in the Gospel History, how that very curtain, or its successor in the restored Temple, split of its own accord from top to bottom, at the moment of Christ's last breath; how, just when Jesus was saying, with a loud cry, *Father, into Thy hands I commend my spirit*, the veil of the temple was rent in twain from the top to the bottom. I can believe that. That sign was just what ought to have been, if Moses wrote of Christ[2], and if the Law was in any sense the schoolmaster to the Gospel[3]. And here the Apostle to the Hebrews interprets for us that rent veil; telling us what it meant, and how to use it.

[1] 1 Kings viii. 46.   [2] John v. 46.   [3] Gal. iii. 24.

Having therefore, brethren, boldness to enter into the holiest by the blood of Jesus.

Boldness, he says. Not audacity, but confidence: that freedom and frankness of utterance which a slave has not before his tyrant, but which a dutiful subject, a respectful servant, a loving child has before his Sovereign, before his Master, before his Father. That freedom of speech which springs out of reverence and gratitude and love combined; which hides nothing, because all is known, and because the worst that can be told only makes the speaking more needful and the confidence more blessed and more assured. Have you some secret upon your soul—something which you would not breathe to your nearest and your most dear? O get rid of it as a secret, by breathing it into the ear of Him who is at once Omniscient—aware of it already—and yet tenderly loving, and yet strong to save!

Boldness for the entering of the holiest. That veil which kept out all inferior Priests, even those who lighted the lamps and changed the shewbread—that veil which excluded even the High Priest every day of the year save one—need not keep out you. Under Christ, you, Christian man, Christian woman, are your own High Priest. Push aside the dividing Veil, and enter.

But what shall you take with you? The High Priest must take with him the incense beaten small, and the censer of coals from the great brasen altar. He must take with him also—*that he die not*[1]—the bowl of

---

[1] Lev. xvi. 13.

blood from the bullock and the goat of the sin-offering. What must you take?

You are to enter *by (in) the blood of Jesus*. I know not how we could have had more strongly impressed upon us the solemn, the august importance of that amazing act of Sacrifice, by which our Lord Jesus Christ gave Himself for the sins of the world. Whenever we use our sacerdotal privilege of entering God's Presence, we must do so *in the blood of Jesus*—on the strength of what He has done for us—in virtue of His Death. O, while God speaks of it in this way, I can be content to wait! Perhaps we shall know—or perhaps we shall never know—exactly how Christ atoned. Meanwhile, I shall be careful to take with me the Blood! I will not risk rejection, I will not incur the charge of presumption, by pushing aside that Curtain till I am sure that I have the Blood—that is, except in firm reliance upon the Atonement, mysterious yet necessary, of our Lord Jesus Christ. I do not see that God explains to me, or that God will blame me for not understanding without Him, exactly how the Death of Jesus Christ atoned for my sin: but I do see that He everywhere speaks of it as something real, something which He expects me to rely upon, even because He Himself has revealed it to me.

I hold in my hand the bason of sacrificial blood—in other words, I have in my heart a firm reliance upon what Jesus Christ did for me, in bearing my sins—I approach the Veil—how?

The Apostle says, *By a new and a living way which Christ consecrated for us.* Every step is on holy ground.

And that ground which is all holy, because it is all God's, needs a special consecration and dedication for the sinner. Heaven itself, we read in the 9th chapter, though pure in itself, as being God's Presence, yet needed a relative purification[1], that is, a consecration for man's entrance: therefore not only the end, but the way, was all dedicated for us and inaugurated by Jesus Christ: each step of the first approach, and each step of each day's approach, to God's Mercy-seat, must be taken on the strength of what Christ has done for us. The way by which we draw nigh is also a *new* way; not the old way of forms and ceremonies, but a spiritual way, paved in the heart, and issuing in God's Presence. And it is a *living* way; one in which dead victims are valueless as dead works[2]; one in which nothing avails but the offering of a life—Christ's life first, our life afterwards and for ever.

Now this way—this new and living way—I want to find, I want to keep it: in which direction does it lie? how can I make sure of entering upon, how of keeping it?

See you that Veil—that Curtain, of which we have said so much—hanging there, not outside the first door—you have passed inside that—but between the two chambers of the Tabernacle? Yes:—What is that Veil? It is, the Apostle says, *His flesh;* the human nature of our Lord Jesus Christ.

O, how much do we owe to the Incarnation of Jesus Christ! What a vague, impalpable, intangible thing, to the carnal, unspiritual, fallen man, is the pure and glorious Divinity! *No man,* Scripture says, *hath seen*

---

[1] Heb. ix. 23.   [2] Heb. ix. 14.

God at any time[1]: *no man*, Scripture says again, *hath seen or can see Him*[2]: we know that He is, and that He is great and good and Omnipotent and Omnipresent—but what of that? I am not great and good—how can I draw nigh to Him?

Well then, God knew this difficulty, this inaccessibility of the Infinite to the finite—and what has He done? Look again at that Veil. You may think that it divides, but it really forms a link between you and your God. That Veil, that Curtain, is the Humanity of Jesus Christ. He took our nature upon Him, that in it He might feel, that in it He might be tempted, that in it He might suffer, that in it He might die. Draw nigh to Him in it—approach the Veil which is His Flesh, and you will be at the very door, at the very entrance, of the Heaven of the Invisible and the Self-existent. Push aside that Veil—or rather, enter through it, through Jesus Christ as made for you very Man—and you are in God's Presence at once. That august shrine and presence-chamber, which only one man could see in each generation—he only once a year, he only in figure and type—you can enter, not familiarly indeed yet boldly, without concealment, without a secret, as often as you will, in the Blood of Jesus, and through the Veil which is His Flesh.

I said indeed that every Christian man is a High Priest. It is so. The Apostle says this in plain words here. But it is not that he takes Christ's place. He is not his own High Priest in the sense in which Christ is the High Priest of man. No. He takes Christ's blood

[1] John i. 18.   [2] 1 Tim. vi. 16.

with him when he goes in. So far Christ is the Victim, the Sacrifice, once offered, never again to bleed or suffer or die, long as the world stands, long as eternity endures. But the 21st verse says this:—You are not independent High Priests, even with the Sacrifice, even with the Blood. No, you have still a High Priest—or rather, *a great (mighty) Priest*—over the House of God. Ill were it for us if it were not so! Even the all-sufficient Sacrifice would be none, unless the Divine Victim lived, unless the Divine Victim were also the Immortal Priest. It is the Life after death which gives efficacy even to the Death. It is the presence of the mighty Priest in Heaven which makes the entering of the Holies possible for man below. Christ the Sacrifice is also Christ the Priest, Christ the Intercessor, and Christ the Life.

O, my brethren, we are well equipped and furnished for the Divine life proposed to us. Then *let us draw near*. The original says, *Let us keep drawing near*. It is not one act to which we are called. It is a repetition, it is a perpetuity, of acts of approach. This is our life. To be always drawing near. In acts of worship—of public prayer and praise, and edification and communion. But not thus only. This House of God—beautiful, majestic, august as it is—cannot supersede the more spiritual one. The heart is the shrine. There, then, let us be drawing near. *In the evening, and morning, and at noon-day, will I pray, and that instantly*[1]. And at special times and seasons also. When I am in heaviness, in loneliness, in sorrow. When I feel myself neglected,

[1] Psalm lv. 17.

outcast, spurned by those I love, then let me draw near to One who never despises. And when the tempter is very near to me—when I hear his footstep, when I feel his breath, when he whispers to me, *It is written*[1]—*Thou shalt not surely die*[2]—then let me draw nigh. Satan never passes that Veil, which is the Flesh of Christ. He remembers too well, too vividly, what he suffered from it once below: the bruise in his head[3], once received from it, is never forgotten. Take the Blood, go within the Veil—Satan will not follow you. And when death approaches, O, then—then more literally, then above all—draw near with a true heart, and you shall find rest for ever.

Yes, *with a true heart*—that there must be—and also *a full assurance of faith*. Of course you cannot go through that Curtain, unless you have the Blood with you, unless you know what the Veil is, unless you believe Who dwells within. But perhaps you have not this. You are a timid doubting person. You have a spark of faith—you can say, *To whom else shall I go?*—but you have no conviction, no confidence, nothing to be called full assurance. O, my brethren, it is a great mercy to know that Jesus Christ *breaks not the bruised reed, quenches not* even *the smouldering flax*[4]. I never heard of any one whom He shut out. He judges of Faith, not so much by what a man feels, as by what he does. If He sees a man trying to get to the Veil, making for the Veil, however tottering or vacillating be the steps, He never repulses, He never pushes him aside! Desire to get through the Veil, resolve to get through the Veil—

[1] Matt. iv. 6.   [2] Gen. iii. 6.   [3] Gen. iii. 15.   [4] Matt. xii. 20.

and you have faith enough for acceptance, enough for safety, if not enough for happiness or for triumph or for transport!

Just two words more.

We have spoken of the Christian as a High Priest. The Christian life is that—the life of one of God's dedicated, set-apart, consecrated ones. There are two parts in that consecration. There were two parts in the Aaronic consecration[1]. The last words of the text express them. There is first the *heart sprinkled from*—that is, *so as to take away—an evil conscience.* What is an evil conscience? It is a conscience all blotted and disfigured and distressed by guilt unforgiven and by sin unsubdued. We cannot separate these two things; though, theologically, they are distinguished into the justifying and the sanctifying. But we take St John's words very broadly when he says, *The blood of Jesus Christ His Son cleanseth us from all sin.* We do not believe in a forgiveness which brings with it no holiness. We do not believe in it because we see no comfort in it, and because we are sure that God, who *is not mocked*[2], does not mock. Therefore we take *the blood of sprinkling*[3], that is, the blood of Christ's Cross, as carrying with it, in one, two virtues—the virtue of the forgiving, and the virtue of the cleansing. Be sure, where one is, there is the other. There may be a ghost or a counterfeit of either alone: but where one is really, there is the other. And surely, surely, it is well so! This makes the Gospel a sound, not a fantastic thing; a power and a life, not a jest and a mockery.

Then the High Priest has this first—the consecrating

---

[1] Exod. xxix. 4, 20.   [2] Gal. vi. 7.   [3] Heb. xii. 24.

Blood. He believes in Jesus Christ, and is forgiven; he believes in Jesus Christ, and is made clean. Comfort him not—which is, in other words, delude him not—with a forgiveness which is no sanctification, with a relief from punishment, which is not also an escape from sin!

And then, finally, there is the *washing of the body* with the baptismal water. A light and easy thing in these days; when the little child, passive and unintelligent, is brought, as of course, to the consecrating stream. Not of course in old days; when the Baptism of water was oftentimes also a Baptism of blood. Therefore we must see that the real thing go along, in us, with the typical. We must see that *the answer of a good conscience* follow, if it could not accompany, *the putting away of the filth of the flesh*[1]*;* that ours be that mind of the baptized, that penitent, that believing mind, without which the water is a form, or, if not wholly a form, yet rather a condemnation than a blessing!

So let us keep our Holy Week, with thoughts altogether sober and wholesome and solemn! Let us try, let us labour, let us watch, let us pray, that we may draw out of this great, this awful commemoration its deepest, highest, most spiritual good; and so pass through the Cross and through the Grave of Jesus, to that blessed Easter, that glorious Resurrection-day, which shall knit together all the redeemed in everlasting fellowship and union before the throne of God!

[1] 1 Pet. iii. 21.

MONDAY BEFORE EASTER,
March 22, 1869.

III.

LOVE NOT THE WORLD.

1 JOHN ii. 15.

Love not the world.

WHEN St Paul said that by the Cross of Jesus Christ *the world was crucified to him and he to the world*[1]; when his Master said, summing up at its close the whole work, the whole achievement, of His earthly being,
I have overcome the world[2];
this brief charge which I have read to you—
Love not the world—
was made by these utterances, not only a suitable text for Passion Week, but also, rightly understood, the very sum and substance of all that this sacred season has to say to us in the way *of doctrine, of reproof, of correction, of instruction in righteousness*[3].

Give yourselves, with me, my brethren, this night, diligently to ponder, and earnestly to appropriate this holy lesson of St John,
Love not the world.
The tone of the words is emphatic; and the sense, on a first hearing, plain.

The World—the *Love of the World*—the prohibition

---

[1] Gal. vi. 14. [2] John xvi. 33. [3] 2 Tim. iii. 16.

of *the Love of the World*—who does not apprehend, who does not recognize, the thing spoken of, and the rule laid down concerning it?

Christians all admit that to be worldly is wrong. To call a man worldly is to reproach him. It is almost to say that he is not a Christian. So thoroughly is the text accepted as a principle, as a maxim, of the Gospel.

And yet how different, how opposite, are the senses in which men have read, are reading, will to the end read, this brief saying!

The world—how vague, how dim, how capricious, our idea of it! How few mean by it their own world!

And *the love of the world*—how far off from ourselves do we place the sentiment expressed by it! Into how visionary a region do we dismiss the affection, the attachment, the passion, to which alone we make the term applicable!

And the prohibition, consequently—the saying, *Love not the world*—Feel not this improbable affection for this visionary thing—what has become of it, by this time, as a reality for ourselves? Where is its bite or its sting for the conscience of the most scrupulous? Who accuses himself definitely of its transgression, or knows in which direction to set his face that he may keep it in the future?

Love not the world.

We have two words before us—the one constant in sense, the other variable. What *the World* is, as St John here uses it, demands enquiry: what Love is, needs none. Love is a primary element of our being: there are not even two kinds of it. It is the object, which modifies it.

The love of Man and the love of God differ only in the object. That love of the World, which is here forbidden us, is the same love, in the feeling and in the heart, which, in other applications, is elsewhere commanded. The word is the same which, in its equivalent rendering *Charity*, gives the key-note to that most eloquent, most musical, of Scripture panegyrics, the 13th chapter of St Paul's 1st Epistle to the Corinthians. *Love not the world*, is, *Have no charity for it.* Feel not towards it that feeling, cherish not towards it that mind, which, towards other things or other persons, is the very grace of charity: be not towards it longsuffering, be not tolerant, be not hopeful, be not enduring[1]: cast it out of your regard, out of your belief, out of your kindness, out of your sympathy: make war with it, make no truce with it and no covenant: take it for your foe, let your heart have no pity for it, no forbearance, no charity.

We are driven back, then, to the question, what is this *World*, which is to be the excepted thing, the one excepted thing, from the universal duty of loving?

And it becomes the more necessary to ask this question and to answer it, when we call to mind that this very love, which is forbidden to us as Christians, is, in name at least, the very love which God feels: for the terms are the same, both one and other, in the two Scripture phrases—*God loved the world*[2]—so loved that He gave Christ for it; and, *Love not the world*—for *if any man love the world, the love of the Father is not in him.*

There are two senses, and but two, of the term *World*

---

[1] See 1 Cor. xiii. 7.   [2] John iii. 16.

in Scripture, which could possibly come into competition in connection with the text before us. Both are familiar to the students of St John.

The first of these is, the Universe of created Being. When Christ is said to *come into the world* by Incarnation, and when He is said to *leave the world*[1] by Ascension, it is in this meaning. He, the Divine Creator, was no part of the Universe made. It was necessary that a link with it should be found for Him, a connection which before was not, when He *took upon Him to deliver man*. That link was the Virgin Mother—the clothing with man's flesh—the bringing into one Person with the Eternal Godhead the mortal body and the reasonable soul of a Man; and in that flesh, and with that soul, submitting to act, and submitting to suffer, as One who belonged to, and was contained in, the world which Himself had made. *I came forth from the Father, and am come into the world: again I leave the world, and go to the Father.* *The World*, in this use, is the Universe of created Being.

Will the saying, *Love not the world*, have an adequate scope in this application?

Something, certainly, it might teach us. Set not your affection on things that are seen. *The things which are seen are temporal*[2]. Grasp not with too eager a hand, use not with too keen an enjoyment, that universe of matter from which death must sever you—which, for you at least, must perish with the using. You cannot indeed too much admire, you cannot too earnestly study, you cannot too minutely investigate,

---

[1] John xvi. 28.   [2] 2 Cor. iv. 18.

the wonders and glories of God's handywork; you cannot pursue with too resolute a step the turnings and windings, the heights and the depths, of that mystery of the Divine arrangement which we mean, or ought to mean, by Nature: these things are all of God, and He has revealed Himself in them. Yet even here you tread, in some ways, on perilous ground. The love of the Cosmos—the word is naturalized in English—may become an idolatry. When you look up to the sky, you may (as the Lawgiver wrote) *be driven to worship*[1]. The observation of order may obscure the thought of will. The student of Science may degenerate—he need not—into a Materialist. The lover of Truth has sometimes—not because, we say, but although, he was so—fallen into doubt or denial of the Truth. The man whose soul demands a living God for his Friend and for his Comforter has lost himself in that dreary region of mechanical necessity in which life itself is but the toiling, drudging bondslave of systems which cannot feel and laws which cannot love. The maxim, *Love not the world*, even if the world be Nature, Creation as God made, the Universe as God upholds it, says this at least to us, *Love not so as to forget Him in it: see Him in all, and let the soul kneel while the mind explores.*

Or if ever, not through Science but from a simpler motive still, you should find yourself clinging too tenaciously to the Universe of things seen; should be tempted to say, as some beautiful natures have said, *I cannot*

---

[1] Deut. iv. 19.

bear to leave this bright world, with its skies and its seas, its flowers and landscapes, its glories and its harmonies, and to think of a state in which there shall be nothing but the spiritual; then let St John's words come into your heart with a truer and a more trustful feeling: correct the love of the World by the thought of the Mind which planned and the Power which ordered it: wait for the unveiling of a scene fairer and more beautiful and more satisfying still: say to yourself, in words not more of soothing comfort than of convincing truth,

> *O God! O Good beyond compare!*
> *If thus Thy meaner works are fair,*
> *If thus Thy bounties gild the span*
> *Of ruined earth and sinful man,*
> *How glorious must the mansion be*
> *Where Thy redeemed shall dwell with Thee!*

Or if, yet once more, it be, not Nature, but human affection, which binds you to the present; if your thought is, *What will that other world be to me, of which it is written that there* they neither marry nor are given in marriage[1], *as though to bid us expect no special ties, no individual recognitions, but rather one equal, unselfish, self-forgetting affection in which at present I can see neither sparkle nor satisfaction;* if this be the form in which the Cosmos binds you to the present, and would forbid you to look either with longing or with toleration towards that *new heaven and new earth*

---

[1] Luke xx. 35.

wherein dwelleth righteousness[1], then let the thought come to you, *Trust Him who has done the greater to do the less; trust Him who has reopened to you through the Sacrifice of His Son a lost Heaven, to make that Heaven satisfying and delightful: love not the world as though it were your all; let Him who made, also fill, every part, every chamber, of your being: the things which are seen, even in their highest height, are temporal; the things which are not seen, the Cosmos that shall be, alone eternal*[2].

Love not the world.

St John himself shall interpret for us. Hitherto we have recognized an inadequate, though not unjustified, rendering of the precept before us. We could not, in that which has yet been said, give its fullest force to the *Love not*. Now we will give it its uttermost weight. *Have no charity, no tolerance, no forbearance, for the world.*

For now we shall read *the World* by the light which St John gives us, when he adds, as his description of the contents of the World, his exhaustive description— ALL *that is in the world*—

The lust of the flesh,
The lust of the eyes,
And the pride of life.

He speaks then not of the Universe as God made it; not of that Nature upon which God may still look and call it very good[3]; not of the beautiful order, not of the wonderful scene, not of the delightful home, which survives, for us, the entrance of sin and death;

[1] 2 Pet. iii. 13. [2] 2 Cor. iv. 18. [3] Gen. i. 31.

but, on the contrary, of man's world—of the world which sin has deeply infected, of the world which is God's enemy, the world which, to use his own emphatic definition, *lieth in the wicked one*[1].

It is a dark and gloomy picture which he draws of it.

St John makes the World—as he understands the term—hold only three things.

(1) There is that *lust of the flesh* which is sensuality—in all its forms. O, we must speak plainly, sometimes, of the world of man, and of human life, as we see it. That world is in all of us. When we promised to renounce the world, do not imagine that we undertook a crusade against other men and external influences. The world of sensuality is within us. It is there that we must face it. For what purpose was this Lent instituted? To remind us that there is a lusting of the flesh in each one of us. Now as intemperance, now as gluttony, now as a self-indulgence of some yet worse kind apart from the question, *What has God said? is this desire, is this longing, according to, or apart from and against, His holy will and law concerning me?* in one form or in another it is the World which assails us, even when we might rather describe our antagonist as the Flesh or the Devil.

It is remarkable—I know not that it has received the attention deserved by it—that, whereas St John makes the Flesh one part of the World, St Paul, on the contrary, classes many impulses of the World under the category of the Flesh. It may be that we read, in this characteristic of the two doctrines, some distinctive feature of

[1] 1 John v. 19.

the two men. St Paul seems to have made all evil a working of the flesh. He felt that that human body which is at once the inlet and the outlet of all influence— that body through which alone we communicate with other men, and receive their communications into ourselves—that body in which we fight and war, in which we strive and debate, for the sake of which we desire things without, and by the agency of which we so much as breathe one thought or express one idea or exercise one power towards our fellow-men—is *the* enemy for each one of us. If we can *keep* that *body under;* if, according to his vigorous similitude, we can but so *bruise and buffet* it as to enslave it effectually to the soul, and drag it at the chariot-wheels of spirit, day by day and in all things; then we are victors over all evil; then we shall have *withstood in the evil day*[1]; then, having *preached to others*, we shall ourselves not *be castaways*[2]. To have *crucified the flesh with its affections and lusts*[3], to have laid aside the body in the grave of Jesus Christ[4], to be *no longer in the flesh but in the spirit*[5]—this, for St Paul, was the whole of that triumph of which he spoke in the glowing exclamation, *Thanks be to God which giveth us the victory through our Lord Jesus Christ*[6] *!*

St John, on the other hand, classes even sins of the Flesh under the general superscription of the World. Metaphysicians, I suppose, would say, that the one expression is subjective, the other objective. St Paul de-

---

[1] Eph. vi. 13.   [2] 1 Cor. ix. 27.   [3] Gal. v. 24.
[4] Rom. vi. 4.   Col. ii. 12.   [5] Rom. viii. 9.
[6] 1 Cor. xv. 57.

scribes sin as it affects the man. St John describes sin in the aspect of the thing which affects. Whether it be that St John's experience of the personal conflict was less severe, less agonizing, than St Paul's, so that he could look on, with a larger and more contemplative survey, upon the sin-spoilt Creation, and feel less acutely the entrance of the temptations of sense into the sphere of the individual being—whatever the cause, you would be surprised to see how largely the word *Flesh* predominates in a Concordance of St Paul's writings, and how beyond all proportion the term *World* preponderates in a Concordance of St John.

(2) St John has a second term for the contents of the world. *The lust of the eyes.*

I know that this might be made synonymous with the former. The lusting of the flesh is in large part *engendered in the eyes.* But the Old Testament usage is decisive as to the meaning. This is covetousness, as the other was sensuality. *The eye is not satisfied with getting*[1] is the comment of Ecclesiastes upon the phraseology of St John.

Covetousness. The lust of getting. My brethren, I think that in these days we can endorse from experience that saying of St Paul—though it is perhaps somewhat exaggerated by the insertion in the English Version of the definite for the indefinite article—that *the love of money is the root of all evil*[2]. What have we not seen in our days to spring from it? Falsehood, trickery, fraud, malice, envy, licentiousness, murder. I do not suppose

[1] Eccles. i. 8.   [2] 1 Tim. vi. 10.

that any one here present accuses himself of Covetousness. It is an ugly name: we call the thing, for ourselves, by some other. Yet the thing infects high and low—yes, young and old: *there may be covetousness in the gain of a farthing*—yes, look again, covetousness is in all of us!

(3) He adds a third particular. *The pride of life.* Do not suppose that the *life* spoken of is the same thing, in the original, with that Eternal Life of which such glorious things are written in the Bible. The *life* of which St John speaks is the life of this world; that Adam life which is bounded by time; which comes to us with birth, and which dies in us at our death. Wonderful, when we examine it, is John's description of this life of time! He speaks of the *pride*—it is too good a word for his strong Greek phrase—he calls it the bragging, the imposture—I should be afraid to call it here by its modern synonym—the arrogance, the self-display, the lying vanity, of this life. What can we say of this? Must we not confess that this life of the nineteenth century is full of it? I know that it is a large word. Everything which says and does not; everything which professes and is not; everything which struts and parades itself, yet must die, is a part of it. Ambition is a part of it. That rank, that title, that great name, which earth gives to its Heroes, is a part of it. That false, fallacious seeming which hangs about political strife; that vast, towering pretension which *the Question of the Day* makes for its day; that pretension which is refuted by the next century, the next year, the next session, the next event—that too is a part of it. How much more is Fashion a part of it!

Mark, as those not involved in it, alone perhaps, can mark, the tyranny, the lying tyranny, the cruel tyranny, of Fashion: see it rise and fall and be succeeded; hear it deliver judgment upon the rank below; hear it admit and exclude, not by merit; hear it condemn by hearsay, and acquit by look: then carry your thoughts onwards, and place it, in anticipation, at the Bar of God—O, you will understand St John's word for it then: he calls it the pride, the pretence, the hollow boasting, of this life!

Such is St John's enumeration of the contents of his Cosmos; the World not as God made, but as man has corrupted it. The other was temporal—this is sinful. Of the other he might say, *Set not your heart upon it.* Of this he says, literally, *Have no charity for it!*

The same threefold enumeration of the thing that is evil, is seen in the record, in Genesis, of Man's Fall. The forbidden thing was *good for food*—there was the lust of the flesh: it was also *pleasant to the eyes*—there, in so many words, is the lusting of the eye: it was also *to be desired to make one wise*[1]—wise in that devil's wisdom which is independence of God: all was summed up in it, which should be developed later into new and somewhat more pretentious forms of antagonism to the Creator. St John tells us what it was, late in Rome's history: we see it, every day, *upon whom the ends of the world are come*[2].

It is not fanciful to see the same threefold developement of evil in that great counterpart of human temptation which we commemorate at this season. Com-

[1] Gen. iii. 6.   [2] 1 Cor. x. 11.

mand that this stone be made bread—there spake the tempter to the presumed *lusting of the flesh* in Jesus. *All these things will I give Thee*, this pomp and glory and world-empire, *if thou wilt fall down and worship me*—the lusting of the eye was to be evoked in that challenge. *If thou be the Son of God, cast Thyself down from hence*[1]—there was addressed that false, idle pretension of the ambitious element in the fallen, which would have responded to the summons, if *the prince of this world had had anything in Jesus*[2].

My brethren, I know that there is much in us, not in the basest of us, itself not of the basest, to argue against St John's warning,

Love not the world.

Many men say—I can hear them, I can half feel with them—Surely these calls to unworldliness are as unwise as they are fantastic. Is it really to be desired that men should take part in the life of this world with the feeling that it is a dream? Is it not more true, therefore more Christian, to say, *That which thou doest do with thy might*[3]? Be a tradesman, a professional man, a politician, a man of society—be a judge, be a courtier, be a leader of fashion—with the feeling that the thing in hand is important. Nothing will be done while the heart misgives itself, or while the man who is to act writes the very doing insignificant. Hear St John. He says, *Love not the world*. The thing which is sinful in it, do not at all. The thing which is only transitory in it, do as such; do with a higher love in thee; do as

[1] Luke iv. 3, 6, 7, 9.   [2] John xiv. 30.   [3] Eccles. ix. 10.

one who must die; as one who knows and would have it so; as one who has in him the love of God, and knows that *the fashion of this world passes away*[1].

There cannot be in any of us two loves, any more than there can be two devotions. He who loves God with all his heart, cannot in the same sense love ought else. He who loves the world, St John says, *the love of the Father is not in him*[2].

And the World passes away, and the love of it. O, is there not in you a desire of something that shall abide? Do you not care to be something higher and nobler than a fleeting atom in a fleeting whole—to be but drifting down with the stream of time into a gulf which shall make all your past being a nonentity and a nothingness? Surely you have within you that longing for perpetuity which is the very index and pledge of immortality—that resolute repudiation of transitoriness which is one chief argument for eternity?

I know that it is difficult—O how difficult—not to love the world. With how crushing a weight lie upon us the things that are seen—the interests and cares, the hopes and the fears, of mortal being! Tell me not that these things are fancies: we live in them. These things have power to render life itself an endurance, or a delight. If those around me avoid, dislike, hate me; if they so much as jar upon me by their manners, by their tones, by their looks; they can mar, they can spoil, they can ruin my happiness. If that which God has made it natural for me, being what I am, to desire and to seek

---

[1] 1 Cor. vii. 31. [2] 1 John ii. 15.

after, always eludes me; if I am always the one disappointed, outstripped, mocked, in the race, in the competition, of this life ; if no one will love me, or not the one person whom I love ; it is idle to say that these things are fancies: if they be fancies, then all I know is that some fancies are very real!

Granted all this, still, St John says, Christ says, *Love not the world.* If it is hard for you, the disappointed one, to obey this precept, is it easier for the successful? Yet you are willing enough to call him worldly if he cannot—if you think he does not! Wisely does our Lord group together the *cares* with the *riches* and the *pleasures*, and make them all alike those thorns which choke the good seed[1]. Life is not so unequal, so iniquitous, as we often imagine it, in reference at least to the eternal issue. Advantage and disadvantage, help and hindrance, ease and difficulty, are more equally apportioned, more nicely commingled, than we sometimes think them—if we look at the long future, at the immortal life beyond.

To each one of us this is offered—offered in the Book of God, offered also in the secret of the heart—the alternative love of the Father and of the World. Both none can have—either every man. If we will, we may take the World; its good and its evil, its sweet and its bitter, its large promise and its scant performance. We may take it, if we will—we may love it, if we can.

But then, St John says, we can have nothing else. We cannot have the other love—God's love, and the love of God; the one speaking, and the other answering; the

[1] Luke viii. 14.

one opening Heaven, the other entering the Heaven opened.

This is the choice. In it is set before us life and death. Words would but darken counsel. Each heart feels and knows that this is its choice, this its crisis:— this too its freedom—the one only freedom of the fallen: a love we must have, but we may have which we will. Every morning wakens us to choose afresh; says to us, *Choose this day whom you will love.* The day of grace is the sum of these days; and the product of these choices is the immortal man. *The world passeth away, and the love thereof: he who chooses the love of God abideth for ever.*

Let us thank God for every influence by which He guides towards the right choice. When, as at this time, we are gathered by the Church's call to gaze upon the sufferings and death of Jesus Christ; when we kneel beside a deathbed, when we stand by an open grave, when we receive in ourselves the first hint of mortal disease; when conscience speaks, after many checks and thwartings, and brings to the surface some buried sin; when in some moment of quickened feeling we breathe from the heart a prayer often said with the lips, no longer as in a deaf ear, or to a distant Person, but rather as a cry for real help, a longing for actual communion with One felt to be near to us as our own soul; at such times we do feel that the World cannot be our rest, that its love must not be our choice. Come weal or woe, come glory or shame, come joy or grief, here—I must have a Father, I must have a Saviour, I must have a Comforter, who changes not—*a Friend closer than a brother*[1], whom no circumstance can estrange, and over whom Death itself shall have no power.

It is thus that the baser love is cast out by the holier. Not by resolving against the World, but by *feeling after*[2] and by calling in God. Not by self-made distinctions between that which is and is not the world; not by giving up a few amusements, in the Pharisee fashion, and going aside, with a few congenial spirits, into a society calling itself religious, only to find that the world itself, the real world, has gone with us into our seclusion, still to be encountered or still to be yielded to; not by emptying, but by filling, the vessel of the soul's affection—even by receiving into it that spiritual water, His own gift Christ calls it, which shall be in us an exhaustless well *springing up into everlasting life*[3]. Then shall the love of the World be cast out of us by the mightier love of God: the expulsive power of a new affection shall be proved in us, as in saints of all time, by a change as real as it is secret; and for every vile sordid passion effectually nailed to Christ's Cross, we shall receive back a fresh influx of Divine Love, alone satisfying here, because alone abiding for ever.

[1] Prov. xviii. 24.   [2] Acts xvii. 27.   [3] John iv. 14.

TUESDAY BEFORE EASTER,
March 23, 1869.

IV.

THE MORAL GLORY OF CHRIST.

JOHN i. 14.

And we beheld His glory.

THE Week which we are spending in these solemn Services takes its name from Suffering. Suffering wrought to its utmost conceivable acuteness of agony, is the spectacle on which, day after day, in the solemn yet simple Liturgy of our Church—in special readings, various in their detail yet monotonous in their sadness—from Old Testament and New, from Prophet, from Apostle, from Evangelist—we are bidden to fix the mind's eye and concentrate the soul's attention.

It seems necessary, if we would make the contemplation profitable, that we should frequently turn aside to ponder with ourselves this question,

Who and What is the Sufferer?

We all know that the sight of suffering affects and ought to affect us differently in different cases. The rank and birth, the history and character, the innocence, the dignity, the piety of the victim—the fact of his dying by treachery, by perjury, for conscience' sake, to save his country, in the cause of his God—may elevate what would otherwise be the execution of a felon into the martyrdom of a saint, and awaken in the beholder, not the instinctive pity of a common humanity, but the admiration, the reverence, the profound sympathy or the burning indignant zeal, of one who sees in the dying man his ideal of holiness, of devotion, of moral glory.

I do not wish that we should give to the Spectacle of this season no more of our hearts, and no more of our souls, than is drawn from us perforce by the actual, carnal, corporeal anguish. We ought, again and again, to question ourselves about the Person. When Jesus came into Jerusalem for the last time, to be betrayed and crucified, St Matthew says, *All the city was moved, saying, Who is this*[1]*?* Let us devote this evening's meditation to that question. We will assume—we will not prove, we do not need to prove in this Congregation— what He was, what He is, in His original Deity, in His perfect Co-equality, Co-eternity, and Oneness with the One Invisible God. We shall ask, rather, this evening, What was He as Man? in what manner, with what particular characteristics, did the Divine Nature express itself in human quality? what was He, our Sacrifice and Propitiation, in character, spirit, and life, below—that we may both honour Him as we ought, and also set ourselves to follow His example and to walk in His steps?

St John describes, in the brief words of the text, the impression made upon him by living for about three years in the company, in the companionship, of Jesus Christ.

[1] Matt. xxi. 10.

It is plain, I think, that the Glory of which St John here speaks was chiefly, though not exclusively, what we may call a Moral Glory: that is, a forth-shining of Divine perfection, not in the form of power alone, but rather of wisdom and goodness, of truth and love. *The Word was made flesh, and dwelt (tabernacled) among us; and we beheld His glory, the glory as of the only-begotten of the Father, full of grace and truth.*

We know what it is to us to live with a good man; how things evil seem to shrivel up and disappear in his presence; how everything that there is in us of good is quickened and strengthened by the contact of his purity. St Paul speaks of this as (in a far higher sense) the effect of contemplating, and studying, and communing with Christ. *We all, with open (unveiled) face beholding as in a glass the glory of the Lord*—viewing the character of God Himself in that faultless Mirror, which is Jesus Christ—*are changed into the same image from glory to glory*[1]. *We shall be like Him*, St John writes, *for we shall see Him as He is*[2]. The future sight of Christ will complete the transformation: it begins here, in the sight of Him by faith. May it please God to assist us this evening in the endeavour to behold something of Christ's glory; to see Him as He was—therefore as He is—in the perfectness of His character; and so in becoming like Him; in casting away the old self, and *putting on the new man*[3], which is Christ Himself.

I would have you, for a few moments, close the Bible

---

[1] 2 Cor. iii. 18. [2] 1 John iii. 2. [3] Eph. iv. 24. Col. iii. 10.

and reflect upon it as a whole. For what is the Bible, but the Book which pourtrays and which embodies Jesus Christ? In particular, hold the four Gospels in your hand—shut, but well-read—and tell me what is your idea of Jesus Christ, as there manifested, as thence known.

I am confident that you feel, if the words might be pardoned, that His work—the work of His Atonement, the work of His Obedience, the work of His Example, the work of His constructed Church, and the work of His individual dealing—that His work, I say, is the least part of Him. You feel that, with Him as with men also, being is more than doing. To *behold as in a glass the* very *glory of God in the face of Jesus Christ*[1], is more, higher, more excellent, more inspiring, than even to read of a world-wide Atonement, or even to be assured of a personal acceptance. The latter is a fountain of life; the former is a boundless, measureless deep.

We will not try to define the character accurately, or to gather into one poor human taper of description all the rays of that manifold Glory. But we will endeavour to say a few things concerning it—true, however inadequate.

How entirely, how wonderfully, is the Son of God, the Word, the Only-begotten, the Light of Light, set before us in Holy Scripture as the Son of Man! Nothing strikes us more forcibly when we think of Him. It was so unlike an Angel's descent upon a world not his own. *Verily He took not on Him the nature of Angels, but He*

---

[1] 2 Cor. iii. 18.

took on Him the seed of Abraham[1]. How complete, how marvellous, was the incorporation! He was *in all things made like unto His brethren*[2]. When He decided, in the Eternal Counsels, not to cling to the original Deity, but to *make Himself empty*[3], as St Paul writes, for us men and for our salvation, how thoroughly, how absolutely, did He do it! I need not remind you of the outward visible signs of His union with the suffering, with the fallen; not of the birth and the growth, of the infancy and the boyhood, of the shop and the synagogue, of the eating and the hungering, of the sleeping and the waking, of the *seamless coat* and the cruel shameful stripping—not of these things, for they are but the shell and husk of humanity: they make not the life, they are not the man. I would go deeper. I would bid you think how Jesus Christ felt for and felt with mankind. How He went, in everything, to the truth, to the reality, to the very base and rock of our life. This, I think, was why He so much hated hypocrisy. He hated it, you might say, almost more than sin. That, indeed, was impossible: no man could abhor sin as Christ did. But hypocrisy is sin; it is that contradiction of the thing that is, that upsetting and reversal of existences, which might almost be made a definition of sin. Everything which was true, real, natural—even though it was caused by sin, even though it was sin which made it bitter and which made it suffering—had the compassion of Christ at once, because He saw that it was real, and because He knew that it was vital.

[1] Heb. ii. 16. [2] Heb. ii. 17. [3] Phil. ii. 7.

I have thus hastened into the very heart of the subject, because I cannot bear, on such a subject, to methodize and systematize. It seems to me to contain in itself a world of thought—this thoroughness of the Divine Humanity. It seems to express, as nothing else can, the suffering and the struggling, the sympathy and the conflict, of our Lord Jesus Christ *in the days of His flesh*[1].

1. Because He was very Man, therefore He was tempted.

The Temptation of Christ, lasting (St Mark and St Luke seem to say) all the forty days and nights of this long annual Lent[2]—rising to its climax in that threefold assault of which St Matthew and St Luke preserve something of the detail—was a real Temptation. It has no strength in it, and no comfort, and no admonition, for us, unless it were so. We cannot indeed explain to ourselves or to one another, how He who was *without sin*[3], *in whom* (as He Himself said) the devil *had nothing*[4], could have *suffered being tempted*[5]. We might have thought that temptation would fall off from Him painless as well as ineffectual. But we are sure, we are sure from His own Word, that it was not so. Satan has coarser and more vulgar solicitations for the sensual and the earthly-minded, and he has more refined and subtle seductions for the spiritual and the unworldly. To Christ he presented even bodily lures in a sublimed and spiritualized form. If he bade Him satisfy hunger, it was doubtless on the

---

[1] Heb. v. 7.   [2] Mark i. 13. Luke iv. 2.   [3] Heb. iv. 15.
[4] John xiv. 30.   [5] Heb. ii. 18.

plea of saving a life for duty, and proving a Messiahship by miracle. If he bade Him gratify ambition, it was on the plea of avoiding centuries of conflict, and winning a world for God by one concession. If he bade Him risk the descent from the giddy height of the Temple-battlement, it was on the safeguard of a Divine promise, and for the conviction of a sin-ruined world. Such snares, so laid, might have caught *the very elect*[1]. We are sure of this, that they did derive, even for Christ, a reality of meaning, though an insufficiency of attraction, from the thoroughness of His incorporation with our humanity.

And when the devil, foiled and vanquished at last, *departed from Him*, it was but *for a season*[2]. From time to time throughout His earthly life the temptation recurred and was repeated. It was repeated in the form of self-sparing and of shrinking from suffering, when Peter, who had just confessed Him, rebuked Him for predicting betrayal and crucifixion. There was that in Him, or He had not been very Man, to which ease was naturally pleasant and pain instinctively formidable. Therefore He felt the suggestion of love as an attempt to seduce—saw in the human friend (for the moment) a disguised enemy, and answered, *Get thee behind me, Satan: thou art an offence unto me*[3]*!*

The temptation was repeated, in the garden of Gethsemane, when the bitterness of the full-mixed cup was made present to Him as a motive for its refusal, and when it cost Him an agony of tears and blood to gain the latest, the decisive victory. All this sprang out of the

---

[1] Matt. xxiv. 24.   [2] Luke iv. 13.   [3] Matt. xvi. 22, 23.

thoroughness of the Humanity. It was *in the days of His flesh*, an Apostle writes, that *He offered up prayers and supplications, with strong crying and tears, unto Him that was able to save Him from death, and was heard in that He feared*[1].

First then we have drawn from the subject this characteristic of Christ—the firmness, the resoluteness, of His self-control. There would have been nothing in it if He had not been very Man. There would have been no proof, no reality, of virtue, if He had not been *tempted in all points like as we are*. If hunger, if thirst, if pain, if torture, if scorn and hatred, if mockery and outrage, had not been as real to Him, as keen in their edge, as close in their access, as they are to us; then His superiority to them, His triumph over them, would have been merely a scene in a play, carrying no comfort and uttering no call. *Which of you convinceth me of sin*[2]*?* implies, if it has any meaning, not an insensibility to, but a victory over, temptation. The purity, the holiness, the spotless innocence, of Christ's character, is the foundation of all else, because it was a virtue really tried, and under real trial victorious. He who bids us fight under His banner against sin and the devil, is able to say to us first of all, *Be of good cheer—I have overcome*[3]*!*

2. Then, out of this perfect self-control there springs, in the second place, an absolute self-forgetfulness. Self-denial, even self-sacrifice, is an inadequate word for the thing spoken of. It never occurred to our Lord Jesus

---

[1] Heb. v. 7.   [2] John viii. 46.   [3] John xvi. 33.

Christ to think of Himself—I mean, as to self-indulgence, self-pleasing, self-consideration. It did occur to Him, for it was a duty—it was necessary to truth, necessary to His work—to remember who He was, and to say plainly whence He came. Side by side with the most entire self-forgetfulness we find in Him the loftiest self-assertion. *I and my Father are one*[1], was the utterance of the selfsame Person of whom it is written in Holy Scripture that *even Christ pleased not Himself*[2]. You see the consistency of the two. Falsehood, denial or disguise of the thing that is, there could not be in Him that is true. If He came down from Heaven, and knew it, there could be no virtue, no humility, in concealing it. It was a fact. It was of the essence of His work as the Saviour and Mediator. But, when it was a question of claiming, in present exercise, that Sovereignty which belongs to Deity—of accepting that service, of insisting upon, or allowing, that homage, which is of right the Creator's—then He took the lowest place. *The Son of Man*, He said, *came not to be ministered unto, but to minister, and to give His life a ransom for many*[3]. *I am among you as He that serveth*[4].

It was the description of His life. No servant, no toiling, working, labouring man, ever led the life of Jesus Christ in its unrest, in its homelessness, in its discomfort. From early morning till a late evening He was the Minister, He was the Teacher, He was the Physician, He was the Servant, of all. No door was ever shut where He sate

---

[1] John x. 30. [2] Rom. xv. 3. [3] Matt. xx. 28.
[4] Luke xxii. 27.

at meat. No humblest, most sinful, most outcast person was ever told that He was busy, that He was eating, or that He was at rest. *He came down from heaven not to do His own will*[1]. *His meat was to do the will of Him that sent Him, and to finish His work*[2].

3. This self-control, and this self-forgetfulness, led, in the third place, to a remarkable gravity of deportment and to great plainness of speech.

The business on which He came was serious even to severity. The Incarnate Word, on His way to a Sacrifice of Propitiation, had no time and no heart for playfulness. We may read in the Gospel how once and again *Jesus wept*[3]: we never once read in the Gospel that *Jesus laughed*. We read of the sigh of Jesus even in healing[4]; we read of the inward groan of Jesus as He drew near a grave which He was instantly to open[5]: nowhere, never, do we find that a smile passed over His face, or that a sound of merriment fell from His lips. To Him, at all events, *jesting* was *not convenient*[6].

And thus was it also with the plainness, with the directness, of His speech. It was impossible for the holy and devoted Saviour to think well, or to speak softly, of the self-righteous Pharisee, the courtly Herodian, or the infidel Sadducee. It would not have been true. The only thing which could make even a moralist, much more a religious man, shrink from denouncing hypocrisy, worldliness, and unbelief, would be the consciousness of

---

[1] John vi. 38. [2] John iv. 34. [3] John xi. 35.
[4] Mark vii. 34. [5] John xi. 33, 38. [6] Eph. v. 4.

something in himself which would render such language, however just, unbecoming, because inconsistent, in him. In Jesus Christ no such obstacle could have place. He was the Judge of men, as well as the Saviour: what He saw, He must characterize; what He knew, He must speak.

And do we not all feel that the power of anger, of strong disapproval, of righteous indignation, is a necessary ingredient in the perfect man? For lack of this quality, what do we not suffer in this bad world? How will men of bone and sinew stand by and look on while a child, while a woman, is outraged, tortured, murdered! How will an ingenious sophistry invent excuses for diabolical crimes, and a morbid effeminate philanthropy give a thousand reasons why the villain, why the demon, should not pay the righteous penalty in the only punishment which the viler nature can feel! This is not manhood: this is not the Humanity of Jesus Christ.

4. But we hasten over this necessary but less winning feature in the *moral glory* of Jesus, to that which all have anticipated as the crown and sum of the whole—His gentleness, His sympathy, His patience, His love.

He reserved all His severity for one sin—the sin which calls itself virtue—that deep ingrained hypocrisy of which the eyes are all outward. For the sinner, world-convicted and self-condemning, Jesus Christ had nothing but compassion. With publicans and sinners He would sit at the social table—not to palliate the sin, but to open to the sinner the one chance of reformation. He loved to compare Himself to the Physician, whose only business is with the sick[1]. He would sometimes draw upon the experiences of family life, and make men weep as He told them of some erring, straying, exiled son, whose thoughts even in the far country revisit the forfeited home, and whose return, in misery and penitence, will certainly be hailed and welcomed by any father in whose bosom there beats the heart of a man[2]. Sometimes He would picture to His hearers a mountain-side in their own Judea or Galilee, on which the shepherd misses one sheep from his flock, and counts that loss of one reason enough for deserting the ninety and nine in his quest of it[3]. Thus He taught men the practical purposes of His Mission; taught them at once the peril of a sin and the value of a soul; made them feel that there is a worse thing than sickness, a worse thing than sorrow, a worse thing than death; and that He who gave His life-time to comfort the one, would much more give His life to atone for and reclaim from the other.

We can well understand how He who thus dealt with that sin which had no counterpart in Himself, would deal with the suffering, in mind and body, of which He was to furnish the most memorable example. What department of suffering did He not feel for? The hungry, the sick, the deformed, the blind, the deaf—the accidentally maimed, the ceremonially defiled—the father calling Him to his child's deathbed, the widow following her son's funeral, the mother anguish-stricken for her demoniac daughter—for each and for all He had

---

[1] Matt. ix. 10—12.   [2] Luke xv. 17, 20.
[3] Matt. xviii. 12. Luke xv. 4.

a heart of human pity, and a hand of Divine help; bidding all who would come after Him not to harden their faces against pain because it is temporal; not to plead the greater urgency of a soul's disease as a reason for indifference to maladies and wants and miseries of this life; not so to anticipate eternity as to overlook time, nor to forget that He who came to die for our Redemption was also, above all men, the Physician too and the *Saviour of the body*[1].

5. I will add, in one word, this fifth and last feature of our Lord's perfect character—that He never suffered charity to eclipse piety, nor duty to set aside or smother devotion.

Between two days of incessant, unresting toil, in the service of God by teaching and of man by healing, He interposed, not rarely, a whole night of profound meditation, communion, and prayer. *It came to pass in those days, that He went out into a mountain to pray, and continued all night in prayer to God. He withdrew Himself,* St Luke says—and the original gives it, *was in the habit of withdrawing Himself—into the wilderness, and prayed*[2]. At certain times of more especial weariness, interruption, and sadness, He proposed to His Disciples a retreat into a desert place, where they might rest both body and soul in seclusion and prayer[3].

Mysterious as is the whole subject of the Prayers of Christ—difficult as it may be to conceive of Him who is God, approaching Him who is God, for any other pur-

---

[1] Eph. v. 23.   [2] Luke v. 16. vi. 12.   [3] Mark vi. 31.

pose (certainly) than that of an intercourse of mere communion—we yet feel, every one of us, that without devotion the glory of Christ's character would have fallen short of perfection. Little as we ourselves may value Prayer; short and cold and perfunctory as may be our own exercises of worship; we do feel—and not least the least religious of us—that it is a poor, debased, stunted life which is lived only for this world; that even useful business, even works of charity, cannot supersede, but rather increase the necessity of drawing down God's blessing upon the man who would do good in his generation; that there is a height, could we but reach it, only to be attained by living above earth; and that it is the first duty, the highest glory too, of a spiritual being, to be in daily connection and communication with Him in whom he *lives and moves and has his being*.

Thus we all recognize the evident delight of Christ in acts of devotion—His preference of these to food and sleep, to exercise and relaxation, to human converse or intercourse or sympathy—as a necessary part of the perfection which makes Him what He is. We could not regard Him as our Example, as our Lord, as the Very and Eternal Word *tabernacling among us full of grace and truth*[1], if He had not this point of pre-eminence making Him *all glorious within*[2]. We want not only a Leader of assiduous diligence, of unwearied energy, of infinite tenderness, of universal charity; we want One who, while in this world, was manifestly not of it; One who,

[1] John i. 14. [2] Psalm xlv. 13.

coming to us from Heaven, was in Heaven still even while Incarnate[1]; One who *can be touched* indeed *with a feeling of our infirmities*[2], but who Himself, even in the days of His flesh, lived a life of Divine communion, strengthening Himself for His self-denials and His sufferings by fresh and ever fresh draughts of the light and the air and the purity of His own Home in Heaven.

Thus did He *fulfil all righteousness*[3]. Not in His unquestioning obedience alone to every commandment and every ordinance of God; not alone in His perfect performance of every part, every iota, of the work set Him; the work of Atonement, of Example, of founding and inspiring and influencing the Church which is His Body. Not thus only. Rather by being that which is perfect—that which is complete and entire in beauty and glory—in purity, in self-forgetfulness, in truth, in tenderness, in piety. Being such, we can admire Him, we can adore Him, we can aspire to Him, we can call Him in, we can live by Him, we can worship Him. Being such, He is not only the Redeemer who died for our sins and rose again for our justification; He is also our Lord and our God: not done with, when we are forgiven; not done with, when we are once reconciled: but rather the ever-present Friend and Helper of our lives, who shall first *guide us with His counsel*, and then at last *receive us into His glory*[4]. So let us daily think of Him, study Him, seek Him, commune with Him:

[1] John iii. 13. [2] Heb. iv. 15. [3] Matt. iii. 15.
[4] Psalm lxxiii. 24.

and then we too, beholding His Glory—beholding, as in the mirror of His countenance, the glory of the Eternal—shall grow by degrees *into the same image from glory to glory*[1], and *be satisfied, when we awake, with His likeness*[2].

[1] 2 Cor. iii. 18.   [2] Psalm xvii. 15.

WEDNESDAY BEFORE EASTER,
    March 24, 1869.

V.

CHRIST MADE PERFECT THROUGH SUFFERING.

HEBREWS ii. 10.

It became Him, for whom are all things, and by whom are all things, in bringing many sons unto glory, to make the Captain of their salvation perfect through sufferings.

IN what was said last night upon the words, *We beheld His glory*—in that poor feeble effort to catch something of the Divine beauty of the mind which was in Christ Jesus—you were quick to notice one great, one intentional omission. We spoke of the self-command of Christ in resisting, of the self-forgetfulness of Christ in doing, of the gravity of Christ's deportment, of the plain dealing of Christ with gainsayers, of the tenderness of Christ with sufferers, of the piety of Christ towards His Father in Heaven. But we reserved one point—too prominent, too important, to be touched upon amongst a multitude—the longsuffering of Christ under wounds and griefs and agonies of His own; the mysterious *perfecting* (as the text calls it) which came to Him, and could only come, *through suffering*. We have kept this for to-night; hoping and praying that God will make it interesting, and impressive, and salutary, to the souls here gathered before Him, through the fast-approaching Crucifixion-morrow, and through the days of the years of the pilgrimage which may follow.

This, I think, we shall all say—that, considering what earth, and what human life is, a Saviour who had never suffered would scarcely have been the Saviour for whom the heart of man is athirst, would scarcely have been what the Prophet calls Him—

The Desire of all Nations[1].
There is an irritability, there is a suspiciousness, in sorrow, which makes it slow to believe in sympathy, in comprehension. I have found mourners at once imperious in demanding, and fastidious in accepting, consolation. There is commonly, in the language of deep grief, this sad, this discouraging refrain—

You do not, you cannot, understand me.
To be a *son of consolation*[2], a man must have been in some way a sufferer. And seeing that human sorrow is infinite in its forms and in its accesses and in its workings, it became Him who would be the Saviour of the World to gather up into His one Person all the griefs and all the anguishes—or specimens, at least, of all—which any man, anywhere, ever, should groan

---

[1] Hag. ii. 7.   [2] Acts iv. 36.

under. We can quite understand, in this way, why the Apostle says, in the words here before us,

It became God to make Christ suffer.

It is not altogether easy to see why he should speak of *perfecting* through sufferings; why, elsewhere, he should speak of Christ *learning obedience through the things which He suffered*, and so *being made perfect*[1]. We are quite sure that one who could describe Christ as the Apostle to the Hebrews has described Him in his 1st chapter, as the *Son of God*, the *Heir of all things*, the *Maker of the worlds*, the *Upholder of all things by the word of His power*—as Himself, in the language of clear Messianic prediction, *Lord* and *God*[2]—cannot mean to say that there was an imperfection needing thus to be removed, or a want of perfectness needing thus to be supplied. When he speaks of Christ as *perfected through sufferings*, as *learning by suffering*, it must be with reference to two things—the drawing out of a perfection which was there, and the finishing of a satisfaction which was needed by His people.

We have earnestly asserted on former occasions—and may God keep us evermore stedfast in this faith—the necessity of Christ's Sacrifice in its strongest yet simplest sense, as an Atonement and Propitiation for sin. *When He had by Himself purged our sins*[3], is the brief but pregnant account of it by the Apostle whose words are before us.

To-night we would rather view it in the light in

---

[1] Heb. v. 8, 9. [2] Heb. i. 2, 3, 8, 10. [3] Heb. i. 2.

which the text places it, as a necessary part of the incorporation and union with His Church; as the consummation too of that *moral glory* which shone forth in every part and every feature of the character of the Divine Saviour.

Perfect through sufferings.

1. What was the life of Christ but a life of suffering?

Perhaps you will point to a tranquil Home, an untroubled Youth, the anxious, devoted, reverent nurture of a saintly Mother's love. You will urge that, for thirty years of a life reaching but to thirty and three, we read of nothing hostile, nothing precarious, nothing unrestful. You will add, that of those trials which make so large a chapter of human woe—loss of friends, of parents, of wife or child—Jesus Christ had no experience ever below. You might draw the inference, hasty but not unnatural, that, on the whole, the earthly life of Jesus was as little a life of suffering as any of which we keep the record. He never lay, so far as we know, on a bed of sickness: He never mourned, in His own family, beside a bed of death: He never felt the feebleness, the impotence, the imbecility, of a protracted, an unlovely old age.

We must grant some of these things, and then remind you—

First, that some sorrows of life are but the shadows of greater joys; that Jesus Christ could not have tasted the anxieties, without drinking also of the pleasures, of a home of His own: therefore, in escaping from certain griefs, He was deprived also of certain far greater joys, which became not the Man of Sorrows.

Next, that some other trials of common human life were quite unsuitable to His office—if I might so express it, to His idea. It would not have become Him to run out the term of existence—as though He clung to it for its own sake—to its *threescore years and ten* or *fourscore years*[1]. There was nothing in earthly old age congruous or consistent with the plan, with the duty, of *the Word made flesh*[2]. In three and thirty years He had done all; had obeyed, had toiled, had suffered, had atoned. His Home was above: when He had done all, it was better that He should be there!

Look then—it is more profitable, it is also more true—at the cup of suffering which He did drain.

(1) I will speak to you of His loneliness. There is a loneliness which vulgar natures feel—a loneliness which makes conscience flame, and goads the imprisoned felon into madness. There is a loneliness, too, of which only great souls are sensible; a loneliness felt doubly in crowds; a loneliness, not of bodily presence, but of unintelligible aspirations, misinterpreted motives, and crushed or trampled sympathies. It was this last which made one of the sorest of Christ's life's sorrows. *He came to His own*—it was true in all senses—it was true as (St John wrote it) of the world, it was true of His nation, it was true of His home—*He came unto His own, and His own received Him not*[3]. When, in

---

[1] Psalm xc. 10.   [2] John i. 14.   [3] John i. 11.

the discharge of such *business of His Father* as could be done in childhood, He *tarried behind* to fill His thirsting mind in Jerusalem from the wisdom of its Rabbis, He was reproved, He was reproached, by her who best loved Him—*Son, why hast Thou thus dealt with us*[1]*?* His answer was accepted, was *pondered*, was treasured; it was not understood, even by her. This was a sample of the life's isolation. *Neither did His brethren believe on Him*[2], writes St John. Even at home He was *an alien to His mother's children*[3]. Of Him, doubtless, as of His type in old time, brothers and sisters said oftentimes, *Behold, this dreamer cometh*[4]*!* If you have ever seen the effect produced upon a child, a human child, by ignorant ridicule given in return for some eager, earnest questioning; if you have ever observed that daunting of the hope, that defeating of the intellectual effort—yet more, that sense of wrong done and pain inflicted; you may have some idea, a faint but true one, of the suffering of the one Divine Childhood, from this single, least obvious cause, its spiritual isolation and loneliness.

You might have thought that this particular source of suffering would have been stanched and dried up when once He was free to choose His companionship; when once He had emerged from the narrow home at Nazareth, and had begun to associate with Himself the future Ministers and Apostles of His Kingdom. To them indeed He could speak as to friends: but what a record

---

[1] Luke ii. 48.   [2] John vii. 5.   [3] Psalm lxix. 8.
[4] Gen. xxxvii. 19.

have they themselves left of the intelligence, of the sympathy, with which they heard Him! Again and again we read, in their own words, He said thus and thus; but *they understood none of these things—this saying was hid from them—they knew not the things which were spoken*[1]. Not until after the Resurrection could He begin really to *open their understanding*[2] to Scripture: even when they saw Him risen, *some* still *doubted*[3].

(2) There was one peculiar trial which we must endeavour to enter into; and that was the perpetual suspicion of arrogance and blasphemy. We remarked last night—it is an important though obvious reflection—that our Lord Jesus Christ, however humble, was true. He *could not deny Himself*[4]. He could not, to win acceptance—He could not, to avoid reproach—forget or disguise His own Origin. He who knew that He was *from above*, could not pretend to be *from beneath*[5]; He who knew that *God was His Father*[6], could not even seem to say that, before He was born, He was not[7]. Hence a special distress, not always thought of as it should be.

In these days it is not altogether penal to be heterodox. We have reached an age of the Church, in which boldness of speech, originality of thought, power (it is sometimes called) of mind, is esteemed far above its value, far above truth. The one thing which a Preacher, which a Writer, has to dread—if he would succeed, if

---

[1] Luke xviii. 34.   [2] Luke xxiv. 45.   [3] Matt. xxviii. 17.
[4] 2 Tim. ii. 13.   [5] John viii. 23.   [6] John v. 18.
[7] John i. 15. viii. 58.

he would be listened to—is the charge of tameness, of commonplaceness, of dulness. Better, we say, smart error than modest truth. Therefore we can scarcely estimate the pang which a charge of heresy, much more of presumption, struck into the heart of *the elders;* men who feared God, and *walked humbly, mournfully, before the Lord of Hosts*[1]. To be accused of arrogance, of falsehood, of blasphemy, of being in league with the devil, of doing His mighty works by the help of God's enemy[2], was a trouble, was a sorrow to Jesus Christ, of which meaner, commoner, vainer minds can have no conception.

I put these sufferings far above toil, above hunger, above homelessness, for Jesus; touchingly, pathetically, as He spoke even of this last, when He said to one who would follow Him—

The foxes have holes, and the birds of the air have nests; but the Son of Man hath not where to lay His head[3].

(3) And we must add one more to these sorrows of the life—beyond loneliness, beyond reproach, in its bitterness—the sense of actual treachery lurking in His little fold; the presence of one malign influence, of one perfidious friendship, of one soul (amongst the innermost Twelve) gradually hardening itself into hatred, ripening itself for ruin. O, how must the thought—

Have not I chosen you twelve, and one of you is a devil[4]—

---

[1] Micah vi. 8.   Mal. iii. 14.   [2] Matt. xii. 24.
[3] Matt. ix. 20.   [4] John vi. 70.

have poisoned the peace and wrung the very heart of Jesus, though it could not shake the stedfastness of His resolve to *overcome* even that *evil*, were it possible, *with good*[1] /

(4) And yet, my brethren, there was one sorrow wider, larger, broader, if not deeper, even than this. It was this indeed—we scarcely know how to say it—it was this which brought Him down, it was this which made Him take flesh, it was this which caused the life which it darkened. He must have felt it already—He must have felt it in Heaven. *The free gift*, St Paul writes, *was of (the result of, caused by*—strange words!) *many offences unto justification*[2]. Sin brought Christ down —He was *the free gift:* sin clothed Him in flesh, then saddened, then slew Him.

Sin was *the* sorrow. The sight of sin, the knowledge of sin, the presence of sin—the daily presence, in anger and suspicion, in vainglory and hypocrisy, in disease, deformity, leprosy, death—the prescience, too, of sin's consequence, of *the second death*[3].

You may trace up all Christ's sufferings to this single source—sin. It was this which afflicted, tormented, at last crucified Him; it was through this that He was made perfect.

(5) As the end drew on, there set in new sufferings. We are to commemorate them to-morrow—we are commemorating them now.

Some of these speak to all men. The bodily inflic-

---

[1] Rom. xii. 21.   [2] Rom. v. 16, Ἐκ πολλῶν παραπτωμάτων.
[3] Rev. ii. 11. xx. 14.

tions—the hunger and thirst, the mockery and buffeting, the spitting and scourging, the thorns and the nails, the shameful Cross, the long hours of hanging between earth and Heaven, between living and dying, the taunts and execrations, the desertion and flight of His own—human nature can feel thus far: the simple narrative of these things, if it were new, if it were of to-day, if it were studied, if it were realized, would draw tears from hardened men. If Jesus were a Philanthropist only, if He were but an innocent Victim of man's prejudice and bigotry, if He were a Patriot only or a Saint or a Martyr, we should all feel it then. It is because He is more—because He is our Saviour, because He is our Lord and our God—it is therefore that we feel it not.

In reality, however, these things scarcely touch the real point. The suffering of Jesus was not only, not chiefly, as a Man. It was far more, far more exquisitely, as the Divine Man—let us speak plainly, as God— that He suffered. It was in the sin-bearing, more than in the sin-suffering, that He felt, and that He groaned. It was not only that sin was all round Him—that He saw a world infected, ruined, destroyed by it—an Apostle says, *He was made sin*[1]. Think of that. The Holy One was *made sin*. Put it at the very lowest possible point— you cannot get rid of the Sacrifice, of the sin-taking and sin-carrying, which is our Gospel, which is our hope. Argue not—*only believe*[2]. You will want it one day: think again—you want it now!

[1] 2 Cor. v. 21.   [2] Mark v. 36.

2. The text tells us that through these sufferings God made Christ perfect. *Though He were a Son, yet learned He obedience through the things which He suffered*[1]. These sufferings exercised, practised, manifested, left on record, the perfectness which was in Him.

(1) Was there ever sorrow like His sorrow, or suffering like His suffering, in its submissiveness?

A dying Bishop asked his Chaplain, *Have you ever preached a Sermon on the text, Thy will be done? How did you explain it?* When the other replied—*Just so*, he said; *that is the meaning:* and added, in a voice choked with tears, *But it is hard—very hard sometimes—to say it.*

Christ did say it. *If this cup may not pass away from me except I drink it, Thy will be done*[2]. The cup did not pass—He did drink it: it was the cup not only of pain, not only of torture, not only of death—it was the hiding of a Father's countenance; it was death not only in human loneliness but under Divine desertion: so, not otherwise—not in a gentler form, not with every solace and every mitigation, but thus in darkest, bitterest, uttermost desolation—did Christ our Lord *taste death for every man*[3]. And yet He could say, *Thy will be done.*

(2) Suffering often makes us selfish. The frame racked with pain can scarcely admit a thought save for itself. It seems wonderful to us that all the world is not sorry! Of those who approach us we demand this first and midst and last of all, that they feel for us.

---

[1] Heb. v. 8.   [2] Matt. xxvi. 42.   [3] Heb. ii. 9.

We reject the rough touch, we resent the critical word, we expect every suggestion to be adapted to our circumstance, and every voice to be attuned to our mood. Only Christ, and a few who have learned of Him, could be unselfish in suffering. He thought of every one—thought of the imperilled souls that would not watch[1]—thought of the endangered bodies which must be pleaded for with His captors[2]—thought of the falling sinning Disciple who must be recalled with a look to penitence[3]—thought of the pitying women, whose wailing should be rather for themselves and their children[4]—thought of the bereaved Mother whose home must be provided[5]—thought of the agonized dying sinner beside Him, who must be comforted with the promise of a Paradise opened[6].

(3) Even a submissive, even an unselfish sorrow, might yet be wanting in dignity and in elevation. There have been those who bowed themselves under *the mighty Hand*[7]—there have been those who thought themselves least, and even in dying hours remembered their brethren—yet were lacking in the calmness of their retrospect and in the confidence of their prospect. It was not so with Christ. Whatever the deprivation of conscious joy, whatever the disconsolateness of spiritual feeling, there was no misgiving as to the completeness of His Work or as to the availableness of His Propitiation. Each separate item of prophetic prediction was carefully pondered

---

[1] Matt. xxvi. 40, 41. [2] John xviii. 8, 9. [3] Luke xxii. 61.
[4] Luke xxiii. 27, 28. [5] John xix. 26, 27. [6] Luke xxiii. 43.
[7] 1 Pet. v. 6.

and exactly fulfilled. *Knowing that all things* else *were now accomplished*—all things written in Holy Scripture concerning the life and the death of Him that should come—that there might be left no jot and no tittle of type or sign, of Psalm or Prophecy, incomplete or unregarded, *He saith, I thirst*[1]. And when this too was done, then at last He said, *It is finished*—then at last, in peace and faith, He *bowed His head, and gave up the ghost*[2]. Thus He taught, for all time, the importance of God and the insignificance of the present—the essential difference between safety and transport—the blessedness of all those *who die in the Lord*[3], even though there be, to the very last, neither beckoning angel, opening sky, nor visible glory.

My brethren, the text tells us that all this was done, not for Himself, but for us. It was *in bringing many sons unto glory* that God thus perfected through sufferings the Captain of their salvation. It was to make Him one with us. It was to create, it was to establish, it was to prove, that relationship, that brotherhood, which is between Christ and His redeemed. It was to enable Him to feel with us in suffering, to succour us in temptation, to exercise the Church's trust, and to lead the Church's worship[4]. It was to encourage us to trust Him as our Friend, to use Him as our Priest, to follow Him as our Commander, to live because He died, and to die because He lives. *We are sons of God now*, and, though *it doth not yet appear what we shall be*[5], we

---

[1] John xix. 28.   [2] John xix. 30.   [3] Rev. xiv. 13.
[4] Heb. ii. 12.   [5] 1 John iii. 2.

know that God Himself is engaged in bringing us to glory.

O, my brethren, let us not frustrate this purpose of Divine love. What is *Glory?* It is the sight of God, it is the presence of God, it is the companionship of God—it is the likeness, it is the lost, restored image of God Himself—for ever. It was to give us this that Christ came, that Christ suffered and wept, that Christ died and rose. How are we dealing with this blessed Hope? Where is our earnestness in seeking, where is our watchfulness in keeping, where is our holy jealousy of forfeiting, this glory which a perfected Lord won for us through suffering? Let not this serious season end, let not this Holy Week close—let us not stand to-morrow, on the Crucifixion Day, to see Christ die—let us not presume to meet to say to one another, on Easter Day, *The Lord is risen*—without some anxious questionings meanwhile, some deep searchings of heart, some resolute expulsions of sins, some determined efforts after a better, braver, holier life! Let us not expect, let us not wish, to trifle or play along that road which Jesus Christ marked with great drops of His blood! *If we suffer, we shall also reign with Him*[1]. Suffering of some kind is the condition of our perfection. Christ also Himself was made perfect through sufferings.

Let suffering come, and change, and work, and go, as God shall order. He has charge of us, He chastens and blesses, He can make the very stroke healing, and

---

[1] 2 Tim. ii. 12.

pour the oil of His benediction upon the wound which He has opened. Only may He not leave us, not give us up, not cease to deal with us! All in gentleness, if it please Him—if need be, in merciful correction—so let Him guide, so let Him speed us! At last may we be of those whom He has prepared for His presence—of those sons whom He has brought safe to glory!

THURSDAY BEFORE EASTER,
March 25, 1869.

VI.

DEATH THE REMEDY OF CHRIST'S LONELINESS.

St John xii. 24.

Verily, verily, I say unto you, Except a corn of wheat fall into the ground and die, it abideth alone: but if it die, it bringeth forth much fruit.

It is thus that Christ Himself speaks of the importance, the necessity, of His own Death.

He has made His solemn entry into the City where He is now to suffer.

An unwonted stir accompanies, this time, His visit to Jerusalem.

He had been there as a Boy of twelve years, and no man thought of Him then. He might sit in the Temple-courts, hearing the doctors and asking them questions: no immediate fame published His presence: His Mother must seek Him for herself, if she would find Him: He was not preaching, He was not healing, He was not working then: He was only preparing, He was only learning. He had stayed behind to learn, He accompanied her home to obey[1].

But now it was otherwise. For about three years He had come forward as the Teacher, as the Prophet, as more than the Prophet, of Israel. He had drawn upon Himself, when He periodically visited Jerusalem, first the notice and then the hostility of the orthodox. Again and again He had withdrawn Himself, till His hour should come[2]: now His hour is come, and He is here to die.

At this moment of extreme peril, when the fury of the Pharisees has been inflamed for its last vengeance by the public entry and by the popular confession, there occurred an incident noticed only by St John; an application on the part of some Gentile proselytes who had come up to worship at this Passover, that they might be permitted to *see Jesus*[3]. There was a doubt about it. Philip, to whom they first spoke, had heard his Master say, on more than one occasion, that He was come upon earth to minister personally only to Israel[4]: these Gentiles were outside that pale: he must consult another Disciple before he can admit them.

Whether they were admitted we know not. But it seems that the desire itself struck the heart of Jesus with a sort of vivid foresight and foretaste of His coming Glory. This eagerness of strangers to visit Him, what was it but an omen of the now not distant day when in

---

[1] Luke ii. 51.   [2] John vii. 8. viii. 20.   [3] John xii. 20, 21.
[4] Matt. x. 5.   xv. 24.

a larger sense the *Gentiles should come to His light, and kings to the brightness of His rising*[1]? Without returning (so far as the Gospel tells) any direct answer to the application itself, He suffered His thoughts and His words to leap forth across the chasm of the dark shadow, into the bright glorious day of *the joy set before Him*[2]. *The hour is come that the Son of Man should be glorified.* Human nature might have said, *The hour is come that the Son of Man should be crucified:* but the Divine faith which supported Him overlooked and surmounted all this, and treated the suffering itself as the mere insignificant preface and prelude to the glory.

But He has not forgotten it. The text, which instantly follows, is about *the decease* which He must first *accomplish at Jerusalem*[3].

He looked forward to it. We are gathered to look back upon it. Let us imitate, as best we may, His example, in not confining our view to the dreadful spectacle of the bodily anguish, but rather penetrating through all this to the importance and necessity of His death, as He Himself here lays it out before us.

The grain of wheat not yet sown is a bare grain, and nothing more. *It abideth alone.* Look at it, examine it, handle it: can anything be more insignificant? There is in it, as it lies there, not so much as the satisfaction of the hunger of one living thing. But even the insignificance is not the point to which Christ directs attention. It is the solitariness. *It abideth alone.* That grain of

---

[1] Isai. lx. 3.   [2] Heb. xii. 3.   [3] Luke ix. 31.

wheat is a solitary. While it is as it is, it can never know the blessing of increase, of multiplication, of usefulness, of productiveness. It is just the single grain itself, and it is not, and it will not be, and (except on one supposition) it is physically incapable of becoming, anything else or more.

What is that one condition?

Let it *fall upon the ground and die.* Let it be thrown upon the surface of some field, duly prepared on man's part by plough and harrow, duly prepared on God's part by timely rain and fostering sunshine—there let it lie, till a process analogous to death shall have passed upon it, till it has seemed to decay and corrupt, till it has swollen and sprouted, and lost shape and form, solidity and cohesion—let a season or two pass over it— leave it to that most ingenious, most sagacious, most powerful of all workers, Nature—which is God's order— herself: and then that bare, lonely, solitary grain will have undergone a change only the more marvellous the more it is looked into: it will have become the parent of an offspring: through death it will have occasioned existence to thirty or sixty or a hundred substances like itself: that one grain may have become the very staff of life to a household. *Except it fall into the ground and die, it must abide alone: but if it die, it bringeth forth much fruit.*

The connection shows us the real subject of this little Parable—for such it is—this comparison drawn from a natural process, and applied to the illustration of a deep mystery. It sets before us the contrast between what

Christ was, what alone He could be, before or without dying, and what He became, what He is, through death.

Except He die, He must abide alone. If He die, He can bear abundant fruit.

That is our subject.

The loneliness of Christ upon earth is a thought often dwelt upon. We touched upon it yesterday. While in the world, He was in no sense of it. He was a solitary in soul, even in crowded places, with many coming and going, thronging and pressing Him. The great men, the learned men, the professed theologians of Israel, refused Him all sympathy. The poor and suffering heard indeed with gladness His message of joys beyond, and flocked to experience His present power of ministering to their necessities. Yet even these had (for the most part) but faint and unworthy ideas of what He really came to do for them: even these ran after Him, too often, in the hope of His feeding them by miracle[1], or amazing them by some sign from heaven[2], rather than because they found His Word saving, or His Presence quickening, to their souls. He was alone still, for them.

And even His Disciples, how *slow of heart* were they to understand what He would teach[3]! How incapable of entering into the deep thoughts which filled and possessed His soul! How resolute to keep their own prejudices, whatever He might say; to represent Him as this and that which He was not and would not be; even to reprove Him for being that which alone would

---

[1] John vi. 26.   [2] John iv. 48.   [3] Luke xxiv. 25.

make Him either God's Christ or man's Saviour[1]! He was alone still, even in that inner circle. When at last, on His apprehension, they openly *forsook Him and fled*, they scarcely made the words true, though they threw a cruel light upon them, *Ye shall leave me alone*[2]. He *was* alone. He never really had any one save the Father with Him.

But this is not the sense in which we are to read the words before us. It is not exactly of the loneliness of Christ, as commonly understood, that we have to think now. The grain of wheat is as much alone (in Christ's sense) if it be observed lying in the granary amidst a countless heap of other like grains, as if it be separated from all for inspection by the eye or examination by the microscope. We see what is meant by *alone* when we look at its opposite, the bearing fruit. Christ does not count mere coexistence—the outward presence or company of others—as any correction at all of the solitariness of which He speaks. He might have had even the understanding, even the sympathy, of others with Him— as we know that He had the love, the devoted and unselfish love, of a few persons even in those *days of His flesh*—and yet have been *alone* as He here means that word. It is an aloneness, a solitariness, which may be said to be the condition of all men, save in one relation only: and that one relation is, not the closest of earthly and human relations, but the relation in which the soul, in which the person himself, stands towards Jesus Christ.

---

[1] Matt. xvi. 22. [2] John xvi. 32.

We must draw this out a little.

The solitariness of the grain of wheat consists not in having no other grains of wheat around it. It may be one item of an immense heap of like grains. And yet it is alone till it has fallen into the ground and died. Then, then only, can it bear fruit; then, and then only, is its solitude, its isolation, done with. So is it with Christ.

While He was upon earth, He could have others round Him. He could eat and drink in their houses; He could converse, He could teach, He could soothe or alarm; He could convince, exhort, impress, influence. If He had continued thus to the end—if He had lived to the usual limit of human being, and then died *the common death of all men*[1]—His name and His words might have been handed down to us in tradition or in Scripture, and we might have been called Christians, just as others are called by the name of some Founder of a Sect or a School, the tenets of which are their opinions, its dogmas their principles. But still, through all this, Christ would have been *alone*. This connection of mere teaching, this respect and reverence for His authority, this taking of His opinion for our opinion, or even of His revelation for our Gospel, leaves Christ Himself a solitary still. He had something of this from His Disciples on earth, and yet He continued alone; alone, for all save His Father. This sort of connection is what man has with man; a connection of intercourse,

[1] Num. xvi. 29.

of respect, of affection, of reverence: and yet, as to the deepest matters of all, man lives by himself: *the heart knows its own bitterness, and a stranger*, nay, even a friend, *intermeddles not with its joy*[1]. Like the bare grain on its corn-heap, abiding still alone even in its multitude, there is still needed a sowing and a reaping, a death and a resurrection, to change isolation into productiveness. Christ the great Teacher, Christ the mighty Master, Christ the Divine Prophet, is alone still. It is only when He dies—only when He is *lifted up from the earth*, upon the cross of shame and in the death of anguish—it is only then that He *draws all men to Him*[2]; it is only then that He begins to have a Church and a people and a spiritual offspring; it is only then that He *sees of the travail of his soul*, and is compensated and *satisfied*[3].

See then how little we really know of Christ while we leave out of sight, or throw into the background, the Cross and the Sacrifice! Till this mystery of mysteries is apprehended, Christ is alone, for us; and we are alone, for Christ. He is to us a separate Person; divided and severed from us, far as the nineteenth century from the first century, far as England from Judæa, yea, far as earth from Heaven. There is no such thing possible, while this is so, as converse, incorporation, communion. We do nothing, while this is so, to prevent His being alone: He can do nothing, while this is so, to prevent us from being solitaries among a multitude. He cannot be more—He

---

[1] Prov. xiv. 10.   [2] John xii. 32.   [3] Isai. liii. 11.

is probably far less to us—while this is so, than a Friend whose words we treasure, whose distance we bewail, or whose memory we cherish. At the very most—even if there be the utmost stretch of faith which on this supposition is possible—at the very most He is to us but as one of our human relations, for whom we feel a deep loving regard, but between whom and us there is, of necessity, no actual breaking down of the barriers of a distinct personality, of a separate being. This at the best—O how little likely is it that there will be this!

But now see what the Death does for us—how it ends this *abiding alone*—how it *brings forth fruit* in souls quickened, and lives transformed, enabled, indwelt, glorified!

For, first, the Death of Christ was a real and true *Propitiation for our sins*[1]. We know not how. When we begin to reason about it, we are soon lost and bewildered. When men bid us to explain the Atonement to ourselves thus or thus, they are always adding to Revelation—well if they are not contradicting it likewise! The great and blessed truth, that our Lord Jesus Christ made in His Death *a full, perfect, and sufficient sacrifice, oblation, and satisfaction for the sins of the whole world*, is, above any other, a simple Revelation—a thing which God only could tell, and which we receive and rest upon singly and solely because He tells it. Our Lord Himself, in His great Discourse with Nicodemus, seems to say that the Revelation of the Cross is a greater mys-

---

[1] Rom. iii. 25. 1 John ii. 2. iv. 10.

tery than the Revelation of the New Birth itself. *If I have told you earthly things*—and the things of which He has told are the birth by water and by the Spirit—*and ye believe not, how shall ye believe if I tell you of heavenly things?* of those things which no man can know but He who has been in Heaven? and goes on to speak of the *lifting up of the Son of Man*, that sinners may behold Him in that Death by Crucifixion, and live[1]. Instead of arguing over it, take it as a message from God to your soul. Jesus Christ did, as on this day, bear your sins. You may plead what He suffered on Calvary as your ground of forgiveness and acceptance. Doing so, you will find peace. Failing to do so, you will never know rest: your spiritual life will be to the end *like a troubled sea;* the plunge into eternity will be a leap in the dark, a perhaps and a peradventure where the Christian has his *Yea* and his *Amen*[2]*!*

Now when once this revelation of Atonement is grasped by the firm hand of faith, then the saying of the text begins to unfold itself. This brings Christ into quite a new relation. It is no longer some One outside me—a wise Teacher, a benevolent Counsellor, a kind and experienced Friend: all this might be, and yet I might be alone, as to my real secrets, for Him, and He might be alone, like my earthly intimates, for me. But if He has taken my sins upon Him; if He has borne them for me; if He has had such a foresight of love, and such a power of help, and such an infiniteness of self-forgetting

---

[1] John iii. 2—15. [2] 2 Cor. i. 20.

self-sacrifice, that He actually, while I was yet a sinner, came down from His glory to be made one with me, and in that oneness then for me to die; if He has done this centuries ago, and still, now that I am actually struggling through this tangled maze of sinful suffering being for my threescore years and ten, is there above, not so much watching and pitying me, but rather feeling with me, and pleading for me, and bearing me on His heart there in His glory, making His one Sacrifice still availing, still fresh and powerful, as if it were but yesterday or to-day offered; if all this be so—and what less or else than this is the Scripture doctrine of the Cross?—then, you see, there is a relation between me and my Saviour quite different from anything else that can be dreamed of: He is not alone now, and I am not alone now: He is one with me, and I am one with Him, as I could not be with any earthly person whatsoever. The grain of wheat may be alone while it lies on its heap, or is handled by the curious hand: but now that it has fallen into the ground and died, it is not alone—it has brought forth fruit, much fruit—and I, even I myself, am one little fragment of its produce!

But even this exhausts not the deep saying. *Reconciled by the Death*, we are also *saved by the Life*[1]; the life, that is, after death; the life which is out of the death; the life of the Resurrection and the Immortality. *Because I live, ye shall live also*[2].

This too is the *fruit* of the Death.

[1] Rom. v. 10.   [2] John xiv. 19.

This could not be while the life was the natural, the human being, of a Man that must die. This could not be while He was preaching and healing, setting us an example, and speaking words such as *never man spake* below. This too waited for the Death. Then, out of it sprang the Life; the life of the Intercession, and the life of the Spirit.

O how have we tried Jesus Christ! How have our sins drawn upon His forbearance! How have our coldnesses, our backslidings, our cherished infirmities, our neglected and half-resisted graces, experimented upon the patience and the prevalence of His Mediation! Reflect, on this solemn evening of His Passion, upon the use that you have made of His Cross and of His Atonement. Think with yourselves what sort of gratitude you have shown for that long-suffering love. O ask yourselves what earthly friend would not long ago have given you up; what earthly friend would not long ago have declared you an ungrateful, a hypocritical, a false man? And then think how over all this ingratitude, inconsistency, and provocation, the grace of Jesus Christ has still triumphed—still repairing, still restoring, still bearing, interceding still!

And thus we pass from the Intercession above to the influence and operation within.

If there be any truth in Holy Scripture, there is a direct communication between the glorified Saviour and His tempted and troubled people below. That communication is carried on by the Holy Spirit, who passes between Christ above and Christians on earth, with perpetual messages of love and consolation and guidance, written not with ink and pen, but on *tables of the heart*[1]—assuring them of undying recollection, and conveying into them a resistless strength.

The fulness of these doctrines is for other disclosures; but the germ of them lies all in the mystery of the Cross and Passion. It is the Saviour who has died, not the Man alive before death, who has these things in store for them who believe. The grain of wheat unsown abideth alone: when it has sunk in and died, then it brings forth much fruit.

Wherever there is a soul struggling out of its natural darkness, struggling out of its natural infirmity, struggling out of its natural earthliness, corruption, and sin, towards and at last into the bright light, the supernatural strength, the heavenly elevation and purity, of the new life which is in Christ Jesus—there, there is the fruit of which the text tells. All else may or may not be; but where this is, there is the loneliness of Christ comforted; there is the travail of Christ rewarded by its proper harvest. Let no sense of sin, no experience of miserable weakness, no depth of degradation and wretchedness, keep any of us from the feet of Him who for this very purpose came into the world, bore our sorrows and carried our sicknesses, died at last for us, and for us *rose and revived, that He might be Lord*, one by one, *of the dead and living*[2].

And the fruit spoken of is *much fruit*.

---

[1] 2 Cor. iii. 3.   [2] Rom. xiv. 9.

Already much fruit. We will not speak of ambiguous, of indirect, of secondary products of the Death or of the Life; not now of a Christendom created by Christianity, with all its embellishments of high civilization, and all its blessings of a philanthropy unknown to antiquity: we will go into that deeper and truer world of individual heart and personal motive which underlies and bears up all these: we will say that already—already through the past eighteen ages—already in this busy, restless, self-exalting nineteenth century of ours—Christ has produced, is producing, not fruit only, but much fruit; that the number of truly redeemed souls praising and blessing and worshipping Christ in all parts of the earth is no insignificant remnant, but large beyond man's counting, and also multiplying day by day, and to multiply. The fruit of Christ's Death is already, is if it stopped here, not real fruit only, but much fruit. There are those lying this night on beds of pain and anguish, there are those passing this night along the valley of the shadow of death, supported only, and supported sufficiently, by faith in the Death and in the Resurrection of our one Lord—this has been for ages, this is now; long as earth lasts, this shall be—O let no taunt and no scoff of the unbeliever silence our heart's praises when we would speak of what Christ has effected; let us say, and feel it, *This is He that liveth and was dead; and, behold, He is alive for evermore, and has the keys of hell and of death*[1] *!*

---

[1] Rev. i. 18.

And if even this experience of the past and of the present should ever fail to reanimate the faint and weary-hearted Christian as he toils along, sore bested and hungry, by life's dusty and parched highway, towards what he yet believes in as the land of his rest and his inheritance; then let him open the last book of his Bible, and read there what the *much fruit* shall be when the *mystery of God is finished*[1]—

After this I beheld, and lo, a great multitude which no man could number, of all nations and kindreds and people and tongues, stood before the throne and before the Lamb, clothed with white robes and palms in their hands—

These are they which came out of great tribulation, and have washed their robes, and made them white in the blood of the Lamb—

Therefore are they before the throne of God, and serve Him day and night in His temple—

And God shall wipe away all tears from their eyes[2]—

And then let him say to himself, *The words are true, after all. The bare grain of the unsown wheat might abide alone; but now that it has died, it has brought forth, it is bringing forth, it shall bring forth, fruit—much fruit!*

[1] Rev. x. 7.   [2] Rev. vii. 9—17.

GOOD FRIDAY,
March 26, 1869.

Cambridge:
PRINTED BY C. J. CLAY, M.A.
AT THE UNIVERSITY PRESS.

www.ingramcontent.com/pod-product-compliance
Lightning Source LLC
Chambersburg PA
CBHW031119160426
43192CB00008B/1044